1 & 2 Thes...

Excel in Christ

JOHN A. STEWART

*Lamplighters International is a Christian ministry that helps individuals engage with God
and His Word and equips believers to be disciple-makers.*

For additional information about Lamplighters ministry resources, contact:

Lamplighters International
771 NE Harding Street, Suite 250
Minneapolis, MN USA 55413
or visit our website at
www.LamplightersUSA.org.

Product Code Th-NK-2P

ISBN 978-1-931372-67-1

CONTENTS

How to Use This Study

WHAT IS LAMPLIGHTERS?

Lamplighters is a Christian ministry that helps individuals engage with God and His Word and equips believers to be disciple-makers. This Bible study, comprising nine individual lessons, is a self-contained unit and an integral part of the entire discipleship ministry. When you have completed the study, you will have a much greater understanding of a portion of God's Word, with many new truths that you can apply to your life.

HOW TO STUDY A LAMPLIGHTERS LESSON

A Lamplighters study begins with prayer, your Bible, the weekly lesson, and a sincere desire to learn more about God's Word. The questions are presented in a progressive sequence as you work through the study material. You should not use Bible commentaries or other reference books (except a dictionary) until you have completed your weekly lesson and met with your weekly group. Approaching the Bible study in this way allows you to personally encounter many valuable spiritual truths from the Word of God.

To gain the most out of the Bible study, find a quiet place to complete your weekly lesson. Each lesson will take approximately 45–60 minutes to complete. You will likely spend more time on the first few lessons until you are familiar with the format, and our prayer is that each week will bring the discovery of important life principles.

The writing space within the weekly studies provides the opportunity for you to answer questions and respond to what you have learned. Putting answers in your own words, and including Scripture references where appropriate, will help you personalize and commit to memory the truths you have learned. The answers to the questions will be found in the Scripture references at the end of each question or in the passages listed at the beginning of each lesson.

If you are part of a small group, it's a good idea to record the specific dates that you'll be meeting to do the individual lessons. Record the specific dates each time the group will be meeting next to the lesson titles on the Contents page. Additional lines have been provided for you to record when you go through this same study at a later date.

The side margins in the lessons can be used for the spiritual insights you glean from other group or class members. Recording these spiritual truths will likely be a spiritual help to you and others when you go through this study again in the future.

Audio Introduction

A brief audio introduction is available to help you learn about the historical background of the book, gain an understanding of its theme and structure, and be introduced to some of the major truths. Audio introductions are available for all Lamplighters studies and are a great resource for the group leader; they can also be used to introduce the study to your group. To access the audio introductions, go to www.LamplightersUSA.org.

"Do You Think?" Questions

Each weekly study has a few "do you think?" questions designed to help you to make personal applications from the biblical truths you are learning. In the first lesson the "do you think?" questions are placed in italic print for easy identification. If you are part of a study group, your insightful answers to these questions could be a great source of spiritual encouragement to others.

Personal Questions

Occasionally you'll be asked to respond to personal questions. If you are part of a study group you may choose not to share your answers to these questions with the others. However, be sure to answer them for your own benefit because they will help you compare your present level of spiritual maturity to the biblical principles presented in the lesson.

A Final Word

Throughout this study the masculine pronouns are frequently used in the generic sense to avoid awkward sentence construction. When the pronouns he, him, and his are used in reference to the Trinity (God the Father, Jesus Christ, and the Holy Spirit), they always refer to the masculine gender.

This Lamplighters study was written after many hours of careful preparation. It is our prayer that it will help you "... grow in the grace and knowledge of our Lord and Savior Jesus Christ. To Him be the glory both now and forever. Amen" (2 Peter 3:18).

What Is an Intentional Discipleship Bible Study?

The *Next Step* in Bible Study

The Lamplighters Bible study series is ideal for individual, small group, and classroom use. This Bible study is also designed for Intentional Discipleship training. An Intentional Discipleship (ID) Bible study has four key components. Individually they are not unique, but together they form the powerful core of the ID Bible study process.

1. Objective: Lamplighters is a discipleship training ministry that has a dual objective: (1) to help individuals engage with God and His Word and (2) to equip believers to be disciple-makers. The small group format provides extensive opportunity for ministry training, and it's not limited by facilities, finances, or a lack of leadership staffing.

2. Content: The Bible is the focus rather than Christian books. Answers to the study questions are included within the study guides, so the theology is in the study material, not in the leader's mind. This accomplishes two key objectives: (1) It gives the group leader confidence to lead another individual or small group without fear, and (2) it protects the small group from theological error.

3. Process: The ID Bible study process begins with an Open House, which is followed by a 6–14-week study, which is followed by a presentation of the Final Exam (see graphic on page 8). This process provides a natural environment for continuous spiritual growth and leadership development.

4. Leadership Development: As group participants grow in Christ, they naturally invite others to the groups. The leader-trainer (1) identifies and recruits new potential leaders from within the group, (2) helps them register for online discipleship training, and (3) provides in-class leadership mentoring until they are both competent and confident to lead a group according to the ID Bible study process. This leadership development process is scalable, progressive, and comprehensive.

OVERVIEW OF THE LEADERSHIP TRAINING AND DEVELOPMENT PROCESS

There are three stages of leadership training in the Intentional Discipleship process: (1) leading studies, (2) training leaders, and (3) multiplying groups (see appendix for greater detail).

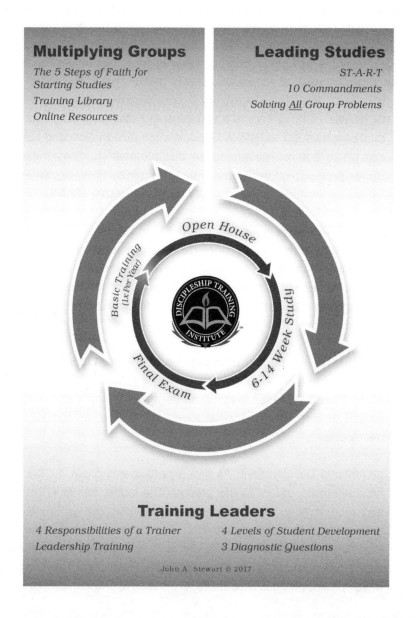

Multiplying Groups

The 5 Steps of Faith for Starting Studies

Training Library

Online Resources

Leading Studies

ST-A-R-T

10 Commandments

Solving All Group Problems

Open House

Basic Training (1x per Year)

Final Exam

6-14 Week Study

Training Leaders

4 Responsibilities of a Trainer   *4 Levels of Student Development*

Leadership Training   *3 Diagnostic Questions*

John A. Stewart © 2017

8

How Can I Be Trained?

Included within this Bible study is the student workbook for Level 1 (Basic Training). Level 1 training is both free and optional. Level 1 training teaches you a simple 4-step process (ST-A-R-T) to help you prepare a life-changing Bible study and 10 proven small group leadership principles that will help your group thrive. To register for a Level 1 online training event, either as an individual or as a small group, go to www.LamplightersUSA.org/training or www.discipleUSA. org. If you have additional questions, you can also call 800-507-9516.

INTRODUCTION

Why do some Christians grow to spiritual maturity, and others struggle to comprehend the richness of the true Christian life? The answer is not a mystery; nor does some magical force arbitrarily choose who will advance to spiritual maturity.

The apostle Paul's first letter to the Thessalonians provides solid answers to the question about how Christians can become mature in their faith. The book is filled with valuable instruction and encouragement, including details about the end times and the return of Christ found nowhere else in Scripture.

Second Thessalonians, written shortly after 1 Thessalonians, addresses theological problems that threaten to derail a Christian's spiritual progress. The letter provides critical information on the day of the Lord—another end-times event when the Antichrist will rise to world domination prior to Christ's return to establish His kingdom.

HISTORICAL BACKGROUND

The city of Thessalonica was founded by Cassander, a general under Alexander the Great, who named the city after his wife, Thessalonike. The city, known today as Thessaloniki, is ideally located on the banks of a suitable harbor near the Thermaic Gulf at the north end of the Aegean Sea (see a map for more specific details). Thessalonica was the capital of the Roman province of Macedonia and a major commercial center with the Egnatian Way, a major east–west trade route, passing through the city. The city had gained the status of Free City through Mark Antony and Octavian (later called Caesar Augustus) because the city had helped them defeat their enemies, Brutus and Cassius. The estimated population of 200,000 was made up of native Greeks, Romans, Asians, and Jews.

Paul and his missionary companions (Silas and Timothy) entered Thessalonica on their second missionary journey (Acts 17:1–9). When their preaching depleted the ranks of the local synagogue and caused jealousy among the Jews, a mob was formed that set the city in an uproar. The mob stormed the home of Jason, Paul's host, looking for the apostle. When Paul could not be found, they took Jason into custody and released him on the condition that Paul would leave the city (Acts 17:9).

Paul and Silas left the city at night, but it appears Timothy remained behind (Acts 17:10). The two missionaries traveled to Berea and preached there, but the Thessalonian Jews came to Berea and Paul had to flee again. This time both Silas and Timothy, who had rejoined the trio, remained behind (Acts

17:13–14). Paul went by sea to Athens, where Silas and Timothy joined him (Acts 17:15).

From Athens, Paul sent Timothy back to Thessalonica to check on the church, and then Paul continued on alone to Corinth (Acts 18:1). Timothy rejoined Paul at Corinth, where Paul's two letters to the Thessalonian church were likely written.

SPIRITUAL VALUE

In addition to the things mentioned above, 1 and 2 Thessalonians reveal God's heart for young converts and remind Christians of the need to walk closely with those who are new in Christ. Paul and his missionary companions went out of their way to proclaim the gospel to the Thessalonians (Acts 16:6–10). They taught them (1 Thessalonians 2:1–4), risked their lives for them (Acts 17:1-4; Thessalonians 2:2), thanked God for them (1 Thessalonians 1:2), encouraged them (1 Thessalonians 3:2), and reassured them about the fate of those who had died in Christ (1 Thessalonians 4:13–18). They also visited them (1 Thessalonians 3:1–2), warned them of false doctrine (2 Thessalonians 3:6–15) and expressed gratitude for their faithfulness to God. Oh, how they loved them!

Paul's two letters to the Thessalonians also emphasize the importance of teaching biblical truth, including sound instruction on the end times, to all of God's people but especially those who are new in the faith. The common idea that new believers cannot (or will not) embrace sound biblical instruction is soundly refuted by Paul's approach to the young believers as recorded in 1 and 2 Thessalonians. When a church doesn't teach sound doctrine, it devalues the life-transforming power of God's Word in the minds of new believers and withholds the truth that can set them free from the lies that previously crippled their lives.

Paul and his missionary companions preached the gospel, and people were saved. The new believers accepted the very word of God and were transformed (1 Thessalonians 1:9). These new believers lived out the word of God, and their lives became a living witness for Christ. Nowhere in the Bible do we see a closer parallel between truth spoken, truth accepted, and lives being transformed.

ONE

THE LIFE-CHANGING WORD

Read Introduction, 1 Thessalonians 1; other references as given.

In 1 Thessalonians chapter 1 Paul introduces himself, Silvanus (also called Silas), and Timothy and offers a standard New Testament greeting (v. 1). Then Paul expresses profound gratitude for the Thessalonian believers' faith (vs. 3–4) and reminds them of the amazing life transformation that took place in their lives. In doing so, the apostle identifies three key principles that will enable every believer to become spiritually mature (vs. 5–10). He concludes the first chapter, as he does in all five chapters of 1 Thessalonians, with a reference to Christ's return.

Before you begin, ask God to reveal Himself through His Word and transform you into the image of His Son.

Lombardi Time Rule:

If the leader arrives early, he or she has time to pray, prepare the room, and greet others personally.

ADD GROUP INSIGHTS BELOW

1. a. What dramatic spiritual event took place in Paul's life that eventually led him and his missionary companions to redirect their efforts to Europe which eventually brought them into contact with the Thessalonians (Acts 16:9–10)?

    he had a vision of a man of Macedonia begging him to come

    b. Rather than Paul telling his missionary companions what he saw and soliciting their cooperation, he informed them what he saw and sought their spiritual input (Acts

16:10). What important principle did Paul remember when he asked his companions to discern the meaning of the vision (Proverbs 1:5; 12:15; 20:18)?

he left at once concluding God called to preach but the wise first seek advise

2. a. Paul praised the Thessalonian believers for their faithfulness to God. List the spiritual qualities he was grateful to see being developed in their lives and circle the one you would most like to see developed in your life (1 Thessalonians 1:3).

work produced by faith Labor of Love endurance of hope,

b. The trilogy of faith, hope, and love are mentioned elsewhere in Scripture (1 Corinthians13:13, 1 Thessalonians 5:8). What *do you think* is the meaning of each of the phrases?

1. **Work of faith** (1 Thessalonians 1:3; John 6:29)

faith and love as a breastplate salvation as a helment. believe the one he sent

2. **Labor of love** (Galatians 4:19)

greatest is love pains of childbirth until Christ is for

3. **Patience of hope** (James 1:6–8)

believe and not doubt

3. Paul's letter must have been a real blessing to these young believers. When was the last time you attempted to encourage another believer, especially a young Christian,

and what was their reaction to your encouragement? Be prepared to share some brief details of the event.

_____

_____

_____

4. The Thessalonians were radically changed when Paul and his fellow workers preached the Word of God (1 Thessalonians 1:5–6). Their proclamation of the Word was attended with **power, in the Holy Spirit and in much assurance**. What *do you think* is the meaning of these three important phrases as they relate to the effective proclamation of God's Word?

    a. **in power:** *He lived among them with power from the Holy Spirit*

    b. **in the Holy Spirit:** *deep conviction*

    _____

    c. **in much assurance:** *they became immitators of the Lord in spite of suffering*

5. a. What did Paul tell the Roman believers about the power of the gospel to change lives (Romans 1:16)?

    power of salvation for all who believe Jews + Gentiles

    _____

    b. Why did Paul make the proclamation of God's Word such a priority when he first preached to the Corinthians (1 Corinthians 2:1–5)?

    he preached what they could understand

    _____

    _____

6. a. God's Word, proclaimed in the power of the Holy Spirit, changes lives. In fact, it is the only thing that really changes lives at the heart level. Why *do you think* more Christians, including some Christian leaders, don't place a greater emphasis on the preaching and teaching of God's Word?

they don't know and haven accepted or understood.

b. What are some things religious teachers preach and teach in place of God's Word (Mark 7:5–7; 1 Corinthians 2:4; 1 Timothy 1:3–8, 2 Timothy 4:4; 2 Peter 1:16)?

their teachings are rules of men teaching false doctrin turn to myths Cleverly invented stories

c. What can you (and every Christian) do to help all Christian leaders faithfully proclaim God's Word (Ephesians 6:18–20)?

pray fearlessly

7. a. Give at least four evidences that the Thessalonians' faith was genuine (1 Thessalonians 1:6–8).

1. *became imitators of the Lor* (v. ___)

2. *your faith has become known everware* (v. ___)

3. *joy given by the Holy Spirit* (v. ___)

4. _in spite of suffering_ (v. ___)

Want to learn how to disciple another person, lead a life-changing Bible study or start another study? Go to www.Lamplighters USA.org/training to learn how.

ADDITIONAL INSIGHTS

b. What three things did the believers in Achaia and Macedonia know about the Thessalonian Christians (1 Thessalonians 1:9–10)?

1. _turned to God from idols_

2. _wait for Jesus from heaven_

3. _Jesus rescued them from death_

8. What specific changes could you make to be a better witness and a more faithful disciple of Jesus Christ?

be bold pray for the lost live out my faith

9. The Thessalonian church was a blessing to the apostle Paul. When Paul wrote to the Corinthians, however, he rebuked the church for being: (1) factious (1 Corinthians1:10–15), (2), carnal (1 Corinthians 3:1–4), (3) immoral and prideful (1 Corinthians 5:1–8), (4) litigious (1 Corinthians 6:1–11), (5) unfaithful to their marriage vows (1 Corinthians 7:1–5), (6) hypocritical (1 Corinthians 11:17–22), and (7) self-centered (1 Corinthians 14:6–20). Paul told the Corinthians to examine or test themselves. What did Paul want them to determine (2 Corinthians13:5)?

examine themselves to see if Christ is in them

10. Perhaps some within the Corinthian church wondered how they could examine or test their faith. The book of 1 John provides a fivefold spiritual test that helps you determine if your faith is genuine, saving faith. The apostle John said, **These things I have written to you who believe...that you may *know* that you have eternal life** (1 John 5:13).

a. Study the following verses carefully. List the five evidences of genuine, saving faith (1 John 2:3; 3:9, 14; 5:1, 4). Note: These five evidences are the proofs of saving faith, *not* the means of salvation.)

1. 1 John 2:3: *obey his commands*

2. 1 John 3:9: *no one born of God can continue to sin*

3. 1 John 3:14: *because we love our brothers*

4. 1 John 5:1: *everyone who loves & the father loves his child*

5. 1 John 5:4: *everyone who is born of God.*

b. Does your faith pass the biblical test of genuine, saving faith?

Yes / No / I'm Not Sure

If you didn't pass the test, or you are still uncertain about your relationship with God, turn to the back of this study guide and read the Final Exam. It will explain how to receive God's gift of eternal life.

TWO

SHEPHERD'S HEART

**Read 1 Thessalonians 2;
other references as given.**

The young Thessalonian believers were true followers of Jesus Christ who pursued faith, love, and hope—spiritual qualities that will help every believer grow in Christ. News of the Thessalonians' continuing spiritual growth encouraged many others throughout Greece.

In 1 Thessalonians 2, Paul reminded the Thessalonians how precious they were to him and how much he loved them. He revealed details about his ministry among them and reassured them that his original motives for preaching the gospel to them were pure. First Thessalonians 2 reveals God's heart for His children and the heart that every true shepherd (and every Christian) should have for others.

Before you begin, ask God to reveal Himself through His Word and transform you into the image of His Son.

Volunteer Rule:

If the leader asks for volunteers to read, pray, and answer the questions, group members will be more inclined to invite newcomers.

———

ADD GROUP
INSIGHTS BELOW

1. Before Paul and his fellow missionaries originally arrived in Thessalonica, they were beaten and imprisoned for preaching the gospel in Philippi (Acts 16:22–24).

    a. How did this persecution affect their continuing missionary efforts in Thessalonica (1 Thessalonians 2:2)?

    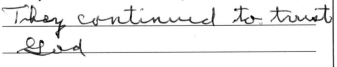

    They continued to trust God

19

b. Many years earlier, the apostles Peter and John were brought before the Jewish council in Jerusalem where they were threatened and commanded to stop speaking in the name of Jesus. How did they respond to these threats (Acts 4:18–20)?

they continued to speak about what they have seen and heard

c. If you are a Christian, what stops you from sharing the gospel with those who need to escape the wrath to come?

Fear

2. The apostles Peter, John, and Paul and their fellow missionaries were so committed to the Lord that they boldly proclaimed the gospel. What happens when a believer is more afraid of man's reaction than he or she is of disobeying God (Proverbs 29:25; Galatians 1:10)?

to be a slave would not be a servant of God

3. a. What things did Paul avoid doing when he preached the Word to the Thessalonians (1 Thessalonians 2:3, 5–6)?

avoided impure motives alert + self controlled

b. List six things Paul did to help the Thessalonians receive the gospel (1 Thessalonians 2:8–10).

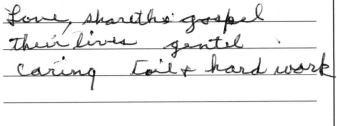

Love, share the gospel
their lives   gentle
caring   toil & hard work

59:59 Rule:

Participants appreciate when the leader starts and finishes the studies on time—all in one hour (the 59:59 rule). If the leader doesn't complete the entire lesson, the participants will be less likely to do their weekly lessons and the Bible study discussion will tend to wander.

ADDITIONAL INSIGHTS

4. Paul and the other missionaries were **bold in our God to speak to you the gospel of God** (1 Thessalonians 2:2), but they were also as gentle **as…a nursing mother** (1 Thessalonians 2:7). How do you think a Christian can be both **bold** and **gentle** at the same time?

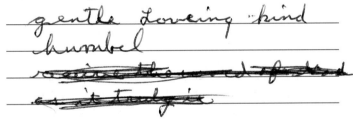

gentle loving kind
humble

5. The apostle Paul identifies two important truths that kept him true to God—truths that can also keep you true to the Lord. What are they (1 Thessalonians 2:4, 13)?

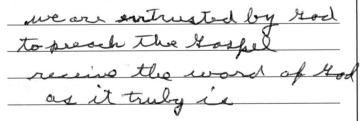

we are entrusted by God
to preach the Gospel
receive the word of God
as it truly is

6. A trust is something of value that is transferred to another (trustee) with the expectation that the depositor's original desires will be fulfilled. Paul viewed the gospel as a precious trust that he must carefully administer according to the Father's wishes.

a. What words and phrases does Paul use to describe how seriously he understood the stewardship of God's gospel (1 Thessalonians 2:4–6, 9–10)?

not looking for mans approval but Gods
no praise
toil hard work
not to be a burden

b. Every Christian has been entrusted with the gospel of Jesus Christ and has been given a divine commission to make disciples of all nations (Matthew 28:18–20; Mark 16:15; Luke 24:46–49; John 20:21; Acts 1:8). If you are a Christian, have you personally accepted Christ's commission to make disciples as a solemn stewardship or trust from God?

authority to make disciples
go and preach to all nations
we have received the Father to g
power from the Holy Spirit

7. a. Paul wanted every believer in the Thessalonian church **to walk worthy of God** (1 Thessalonians 2:12). What do you think this means?

to believe and be baptized

b. Paul also told the believers at Ephesus to **walk** (NIV: "live") **worthy of the calling with which** [they] **were called** (Ephesians 4:1). Paul's use of this same metaphor in Ephesians chapters 4 and 5 helps us understand what it means to walk worthy of God. Study the following verses to develop a biblical profile of what it means to walk or live worthy of God (Ephesians 4:1, 17; 5:2, 8, 15).

live a life worthy

love + sacrifice

live in the light

live as wise

8. Paul said, **For this reason we also thank God without ceasing** (1 Thessalonians 2:13; NIV: "we also thank God continually). For what was Paul thankful?

They accepted it as the word of God

9. a. What important truth did the Thessalonians accept regarding God's Word that positively affected their spiritual growth?

they accepted it

b. How did the Thessalonians' view of inerrancy affect their obedience to God (1 Thessalonians 2:13-14; 1:6, 9)?

you suffered from your own people

Turned away from idles

c. Some people naively think that the Bible contains the divinely inspired words of God and the words of man. What did Jesus say about the Scriptures that proves they cannot be both the inspired, infallible words of God and the fallible words of man at the same time (John 10:35)?

if he called them God.

The Scriptures cannot be broken

35% Rule:

If the leader talks more than 35% of the time, the group members will be less likely to participate.

ADDITIONAL INSIGHTS

23

d. Honestly evaluate your view of the Bible. Do you *really* believe the Bible is the inspired, inerrant Word of God, or do you believe it contains the words of God and the words of man?

the word of God

If you believe the Bible is the inspired, inerrant Word of God, is God's Word the ultimate authority for your life?

to the best of my ability

10. Paul said the Thessalonian believers had become followers of him and of the Lord (1 Thessalonians 1:6). Then Paul said they were **imitators of the churches...in Judea** (1 Thessalonians 2:14). In what ways did the Thessalonian believers imitate the believers in Judea (Acts 8:1–4; 1 Thessalonians 1:6–8)?

They had great joy

11. Paul reminded the Thessalonians of his love for them (1 Thessalonians 2:17). He said he wanted to visit them, but Satan had hindered him (1 Thessalonians 2:18). Many believers struggle with their understanding of Satan and the forces of evil. While some essentially deny his existence, others attribute him with the dual characteristics of being omniscient (all-knowing) and omnipotent (all-powerful). How does the word **hinder** (Greek *enkopto*—to cut in, hinder) help your understanding of the work and influence of Satan, including his limitations?

he is powerful but not all powerful

_____

_____

_____

12. Paul said the Thessalonian believers were his **hope, or joy, or crown of rejoicing** (1 Thessalonians 2:19). He also said they were his **glory** (1 Thessalonians 2:20). Obviously, the Thessalonians' conversion and their continuing faithfulness to Christ brought the apostle great blessing. Do you think your walk with the Lord is a source of joy to others, including the person who led you to Christ?

I trust _____

_____

_____

_____

ADDITIONAL INSIGHTS

THREE

ESTABLISHED IN
THE FAITH

Read 1 Thessalonians 3;
other references as given.

The Thessalonian believers accepted God's Word as the divinely inspired Word of God. As a result, they turned away from idols to serve the living God (1 Thessalonians 1:9). Paul modeled what it meant to walk worthy of the Lord, and the Thessalonians followed his example, becoming a joy to the apostle and an example to others (1 Thessalonians 2:19–20).

In this lesson you'll learn how deeply Paul longed for the continued spiritual growth of these new converts and what he was willing to do to see them advance in Christ. In many ways 1 Thessalonians is a discipleship manual that teaches the extent of God's desire for the spiritual advancement of other believers, especially those who are new in the faith.

Before you begin, ask God to reveal Himself through His Word and transform you into the image of His Son.

Focus Rule:

If the leader helps the group members focus on the Bible, they will gain confidence to study God's Word on their own.

ADD GROUP
INSIGHTS BELOW

1. On the second missionary journey, Paul, Timothy, and Silas left Thessalonica and went to Berea (Acts 17:10) where they were confronted by the Jews (Acts 17:13). Paul left Berea and traveled south to Athens, but Timothy and Silas remained in Berea (Acts 17:14). Eventually Timothy (and perhaps Silas) rejoined Paul in Athens (1 Thessalonians 3:1).

   a. Paul talked about his sufferings when he wrote to the Thessalonians (1 Thessalonians 3:2). When Paul told them he **could no longer endure it** (1 Thessalonians

3:1, 5), was he referring to his persecutions or something else? What could he no longer endure?

afraid the tempter had tempted you.

b. What did Paul do to alleviate his "pain"?

he sent to find out what was happening

2. The missionaries had been persecuted in the Macedonian cities of Philippi, Thessalonica, and Berea. What do you think Paul's deep desire to send Timothy back to Thessalonica, as well as Timothy's willingness to go, reveal about the early missionaries' devotion to Christ and their love for the Thessalonian believers?

the were willing to give their lives

3. a. What didn't Paul want to happen when the Thessalonians learned about the afflictions he experienced (1 Thessalonians 3:3–4)?

They would stay true to their faith

b. How does the Bible describe the afflictions Christians experience, especially as they relate to the eternal rewards (2 Corinthians 4:17)?

it out weighs them all

Drawing Rule:

To learn how to draw everyone into the group discussion without calling on anyone, go to www.Lamplighters USA.org/training.

ADDITIONAL INSIGHTS

_____
_____

c. How can a believer maintain a God-glorifying perspective during a time of affliction or trial (2 Corinthians 4:18)?

what is unseen is eternal
_____
_____

4. What was Paul so concerned about that prompted him to send Timothy back to the church (1 Thessalonians 3:5)?

to be sure they continued
in their faith
_____

5. When Timothy returned from visiting the Thessalonians, he brought good news to Paul (1 Thessalonians 3:6). What three things was Paul particularly pleased to hear about the Thessalonians (1 Thessalonians 3:6)?

1. _pleasant memories of us_
2. _long to see us_
3. _as we long to see you_

6. a. The apostle Paul said **now we live, if you stand fast in the Lord** (1 Thessalonians 3:8). At first glance Paul's statement seems a bit effusive (overly enthusiastic). What does this statement reveal about Paul's heart and concern for the spiritual advancement of others?

he is greatly pleased
_____
_____
_____

_____

_____

b. What do you think it means for a Christian to **stand fast in the Lord** (NIV: "standing firm")?

be bold wittness

give your all

_____

7. Paul was overjoyed to hear about the Thessalonians' spiritual wellbeing and their desire to see him again (1 Thessalonians 3:6, 9). Even though the Thessalonians were growing in the Lord, Paul knew something was still lacking in their faith (1 Thessalonians 3:10). Most believers have one or more areas in their lives where their faith is lacking or weak. Circle the following areas of your life where your faith is lacking or you find it hard to trust God. Things that you worry about are often indicators that your faith is weak in that area of your life. Circle the ones in which you need to trust God more.

your future	family	health
finances	work/employment	children
relationships	retirement	marriage
death	pain/suffering	your failures

8. List the same three areas you find it difficult to trust God. List your biggest fear in each area.

1. _____

2. _____

3. _____

Now acknowledge each of your fears in prayer and ask God to help you overcome your lack of faith. Believe He will help you gain victory over them. You could also meditate on Bible verses that directly address the specific area where you are weak in faith.

9. How does a believer gain more faith, especially in those areas where his or her faith is incomplete or imperfect (Romans 10:17)?

hearing and reading the word

Has your group become a "Holy huddle?" Learn how to reach out to others by taking online leadership training.

ADDITIONAL INSIGHTS

10. Immediately after telling the Thessalonians that he had been praying for them, Paul initiated another prayer on their behalf (1 Thessalonians 3:11–13).

a. Paul prayed diligently night and day that God would allow him to see the Thessalonians again. What else did he pray for them in his absence (1 Thessalonians 3:12–13)?

hearts would be blameless be holy in Gods preasance when Jesus Comes,

b. What would happen if God answered Paul's prayer and the Thessalonians abounded in love toward one another (1 Thessalonians 3:12–13)?

They would not be accepted into the kingdom of heaven

11. The spiritual advancement of others is not merely the result of letters of encouragement and personal visits. Holy Spirit–inspired prayer, such as Paul offered for the Thessalonians, plays a key role in the spiritual advancement of others.

a. Paul's prayer in 1 Thessalonians 3:11–13 would likely have been instructive to these new believers. Rather than offering a rote, generic prayer that was devoid of any identifiable requests, Paul asked God for something specific, namely that the Thessalonian believers would grow in love and for this love to be manifest to others. When you pray, do you pray lifeless prayer that you don't really expect God to answer, or do you pray for specific things for specific people and expect God to answer your petitions?

specific people

_____

_____

_____

b. Now ask God to bring three people to mind. Ask God in prayer right now to show you something specific to pray for each one, and pray for them now.

_____

_____

_____

FOUR

EXCEL IN CHRIST

**Read 1 Thessalonians 4;
other references as given.**

Good beginnings don't always make good endings. A child is killed, a young woman dies from a drug overdose, a marriage ends in divorce, a business partnership dissolves in conflict, and a church holds its final service.

The Thessalonians started well, but would they continue to grow? Perhaps they would fall into the same spiritual trap that many Christians do—church on Sunday and the pursuit of personal desires the rest of the week.

Paul encouraged the Thessalonians to press onto maturity in Christ and to avoid the spiritual complacency that derails many believers. The apostle instructed the Thessalonians to excel in the Christian life by avoiding sexual sin (1 Thessalonians 4:2–8), by continuing to love others (vs. 9, 10) and by leading quiet, orderly lives (vs. 11–12). Paul concludes the chapter with some powerful teaching on the fate of those believers who have already died in Christ (vs. 13–17).

Before you begin, ask God to reveal Himself through His Word and transform you into the image of His Son.

Gospel Gold
Rule:

Try to get all the answers to the questions—not just the easy ones. Go for the gold.

ADD GROUP
INSIGHTS BELOW

1. What did the Thessalonians need to do to grow spiritually and please God (1 Thessalonians 4:1)?

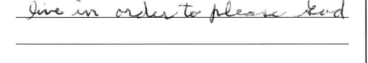

Live in order to please God

2. Unfortunately many Christians don't actively pursue Christ after their salvation. Content to be saved from eternal damnation, they languish in their Christian lives and forfeit the joy and peace that God makes available in Christ.

   a. Honestly evaluate your Christian life. In your relationship with Christ, are you abounding **more and more** (NASB: "excel still more"; ESV: "do so more and more"; NIV: "do this more and more"; Williams: "live this life better and better") in your relationship with Christ, or are you more or less spiritually complacent? Rate yourself on a scale of 1–10, 1 being not abounding and 10 really abounding.

   _____

   _____

   b. In what areas of your Christian life do you see yourself growing ... in faith, ... in love, ... in hope?

   _faith_____

   _____

   _____

3. The apostle Paul told the Thessalonians to abound or excel in the Christian life. Most Christians, however, don't believe they can excel in their walk with Christ. Yet it is God's will for your life. In what specific areas of your Christian life are you excelling?

   _helping giving serving_____

   _____

   _____

4. a. One area of the Christian life God wants all believers to excel at is moral purity (1 Thessalonians 4:2–3). What does God's Word teach about God's standard for morality (1 Thessalonians 4:3; Hebrews 13:4)?

be sancified
avoid sexual imorality
keep the marriage bed
pure

Balance Rule:

To learn how to balance the group discussion, go to www.Lamplighters USA.org/training.

ADDITIONAL
INSIGHTS

b. What is the difference between fornication and adultery? Use a dictionary if you like.

one in the same

5. The pursuit of moral purity is a major struggle for many Christians. Personal sexual desire, enflamed by the sexually explicit images on TV, videos, and movies, as well as the fashion industry's obsessive exploitation of male and female sexuality and a billion-dollar porn industry, have contributed to the destruction of countless lives and marriages and the spiritual defeat of many Christians.

a. How does the Bible describe a man (or woman) who allows himself to be entrapped by an immoral person (Proverbs 7:6–23)?

an ox going to slaughter
an arrow pierced pierced his liver
cost him his life

b. List at least four compelling reasons you should to be morally pure (1 Thessalonians 4:3–8).

Gods will learn to control
your body
not in passionate lust
don't wrong your brother
rejekt God

6. The Bible condemns sexual sin and gives clear instruction how to overcome it. Identify the biblical principle in each of the following verses that will help you regain or maintain moral purity.

a. Matthew 6:13: *not to be tempted by the devil*

b. 1 John 1:8–9; 2:2: *confess our sins He is the atoning sacrifice for our*

c. James 1:12–16: *Confess your sins and pray for each other*

don't be deceived

d. James 5:16: _____

e. Proverbs 5:20–21: *don't give in to an adulteress*

f. 1 Corinthians 10:13: *God will not let y to be tempted if you are faithfu*

g. 2 Corinthians 10:4–5: *be obedient to God*

h. Philippians 4:8: *Think about whatever is true, noble, right, pure, lovely, admirable*

i. John 8:3–11: *Jesus said to the two go & sin no more*

j. Matthew 5:27–28: *looking lustfully*

7. God's people should excel in moral purity and abound in loving other believers. Paul said he didn't need to remind the Thessalonians to love one another (although he did so) because they were taught by God to love one another (1 Thessalonians 4:9–10). How do you think believers are

He sent Jesus

taught by God to love one another (John 16:13; 1 John 2:26–27)?

be guided by the Spirit of truth remain in Gods anointing

8. Paul's command to lead a quiet life, to mind their own business, and to work with their own hands appears to contradict Jesus' admonition to be salt and light and his command to expose the works or deeds of darkness (1 Thessalonians 4:11–13, Matthew 5:13; Ephesians 5:11)? Why were the Thessalonians to live this way?

we have been given the Spirit expose the deeds of darkness to be the salt of the earth

9. Many Christians avoid the subject of eschatology (pronounced *es-ka-TALL-o-gy*, the study of last things or end times) because they don't believe they can understand it, or they are afraid of causing controversy with other believers.

a. What did Paul tell the Thessalonians about the subject of the end times, especially as it related to those believers who have died (1 Thessalonians 4:13)?

he does not want them to grieve without hope

b. What did Paul want the Thessalonians to learn as a result of having a better understanding of end-time events (1 Thessalonians 4:13, 18)?

They are assured of their salvation

c. What does the Bible teach about the resurrection of Christians who have already died and Christians who are still alive when Christ returns (1 Thessalonians 4:15–17)?

The Lord will first those who have died and then take those who are still alive

10. Christ will return to gather all believers to meet Him in the air (1 Thessalonians 4:17). He will come again a second time as the King of kings and Lord of lords (Revelation 19:16). The first time He comes *for* His saints (1 Thessalonians 4:16–17) and a second time he comes *with* His saints (Revelation 19:11–14). The Thessalonians were waiting for Christ's return (1 Thessalonians 1:10), and Paul was ready for Christ to return (Philippians 1:22–23). If Christ returned today, would you be ready to meet Him?

Yes / No / I'm Not Sure

If you are not ready to face Jesus Christ when He returns, read the Final Exam. It will teach how to receive God's gift of salvation so you can look forward to meeting Jesus when He returns.

FIVE

DAY OF THE LORD

In 1 Thessalonians 4:13–18 Paul addressed the question about the status of deceased Christians when Jesus Christ returns to earth. Deceased Christians will be resurrected first, and those believers who are alive at Christ's return will be caught up to meet the Lord in the air (1 Thessalonians 4:17). In Latin, the word for "caught up" is *rapturo*, from which the term "rapture" is derived. The term *rapture* refers to the specific future event when Jesus Christ returns to earth to gather all true believers to Him and takes them to heaven with Him before the beginning of the seven-year tribulation period.

In 1 Thessalonians 5:1–11, the apostle expands his teaching on the end times and provides valuable instruction on the future **day of the Lord** (1 Thessalonians 5:1–11). The **day of the Lord** (also called the time of Jacob's trouble; Jeremiah 30:7) is a future event when God will judge the world, punish the nations, and prepare national Israel for Christ's return. Knowing Christ's return is imminent, Christians should live God-honoring lives.

Before you begin, ask God to reveal Himself through His Word and transform you into the image of His Son.

No-Trespassing
Rule:

To keep the Bible study on track, avoid talking about political parties, church denominations, and Bible translations.

———

ADD GROUP
INSIGHTS BELOW

1. Paul reminded the Thessalonian believers that they had already been taught about the events leading up to the **day of the Lord** (1 Thessalonians 5:1). What do you think it means that the **day of the Lord** will come **as a thief in the night** (1 Thessalonians 5:2–3)?

39

_____

_____

_____

2. What specific words and phrases are used to describe this same event and the events that will take place during that time:

a. Isaiah 13:9–13: _____

_____

_____

b. Joel 2:28–32: _____

_____

_____

c. Amos 5:18: _____

_____

_____

d. 2 Peter 3:10: _____

_____

_____

3. A false proclamation of **peace and safety** (presumably by world leaders and other people of influence) will precede the **day of the Lord** (1 Thessalonians 5:3). The coming of the day of the Lord is also compared here to a woman about to give birth. What truths do you think the illustration of a woman about to give birth teaches about the specific nature of the **day of the Lord** (1 Thessalonians 5:3)?

_____

_____

4. Jesus uses this same illustration of a woman in labor when He described the event leading up to the day of the Lord

(Matthew 24:8). What are some additional indicators that the day of the Lord will be close at hand (Matthew 24:3–12)?

_____

_____

_____

_____

5. Christians often react differently to the biblical teaching on the future events such as the **day of the Lord**. Some ignore it, believing biblical prophecy is too difficult to understand. Some ignore it because they are fearful that they (or loved ones) will personally experience this outpouring of God's wrath. What does the Bible teach about the believer's involvement in this dreadful future time known as the **day of the Lord** (1 Thessalonians 1:10; 5:9)?

ADDITIONAL
INSIGHTS

_____

_____

6. a. How should a Christian live, knowing the **day of the Lord** is coming (1 Thessalonians 5:4–8, 2 Corinthians 5:11)?

_____

_____

_____

_____

b. If you knew that Jesus would return within the next 48 hours and the great and dreadful **day of the Lord** would begin, what would you do with your last hours on earth?

_____

_____

_____

7. What do you think is the meaning of the phrase **putting on the breastplate of faith and love** (1 Thessalonians 5:8)?

_____

_____

_____

_____

8. In 1 Thessalonians 5:6 the Bible says, **let us not sleep, as others do**, but 1 Thessalonians 5:10 says, **that whether we wake or sleep, we should live together with Him** (Jesus). In 1 Thessalonians 5:6 the admonition is to be spiritually alert in your relationship with Christ especially in light of the return of Christ and the coming of the **day of the Lord**. What do you think is the meaning of the metaphor in 1 Thessalonians 5:10?

_____

_____

_____

_____

_____

9. The apostle Paul concludes this section on end-time events with these interesting words, **Therefore comfort each other and edify one another** (1 Thessalonians 5:11). If believers are going to go through the dreadful events known as the **day of the Lord**, these words are hardly words of comfort.

a. In what ways do you think the biblical teaching on the end times should comfort believers?

_____

_____

_____

_____

b. In what ways do you think that the biblical teaching on the end times, specifically God's coming judgment during the day of the Lord, should impact believers?

_____

_____

_____

_____

c. Now that you have learned more about biblical prophecy, including the coming resurrection of believers and the dreadful events of the day of the Lord, how will it change your life from this point forward?

_____

_____

_____

_____

ADDITIONAL
INSIGHTS

10. Many people say that all religions teach basically the same thing. While it's true that many teach a similar moral code, their similarities to biblical Christianity end quickly. Only biblical Christianity teaches that man must be redeemed, not by good works, but by faith in the finished work of a righteous sacrifice (Christ) on his behalf. What would you say to someone who says all religions are basically the same, thereby dismissing the key distinctive of biblical Christianity, including man's need to be saved through saving faith in Jesus Christ?

_____

_____

_____

_____

_____

ADDITIONAL INSIGHTS

Six

HARMONY IN GOD'S FAMILY

Read 1 Thessalonians 5:12–28; other references as given.

The term **brother** (plural *brothers, brethren*) is a favorite expression of the apostle Paul's. Of the more than 60 times Paul uses it in his letters, 27 are found in his two short books of 1 and 2 Thessalonians. The word is a term of endearment, and it speaks of both the interconnectedness and the bondedness that all believers share as members of the family of God, especially as they relate to one another in a local church.

In 1 Thessalonians 5:12–28 the apostle Paul teaches the young Thessalonian believers how to live in harmony with other believers. He explains how to be rightly related to God-ordained authority within the church (1 Thessalonians 5:12–13), how to live in harmony with other brothers and sisters (1 Thessalonians 5:1415), how to worship God in your personal life (1 Thessalonians 5:16–20), and how to exercise discernment (1 Thessalonians 5:21–22). He concludes 1 Thessalonians with a prayer of benediction (1 Thessalonians 5:23–24), a request for prayer for his missionary companions and himself (1 Thessalonians 5:25) and some closing comments (1 Thessalonians 5:26–28).

Before you begin, ask God to reveal Himself through His Word and transform you into the image of His Son.

Transformation Rule:

Seek for personal transformation, not mere information, from God's Word.

ADD GROUP INSIGHTS BELOW

1. a. Name three responsibilities every spiritual leader should assume as an overseer of a local church (1 Thessalonians 5:12–13).

45

_____

_____

_____

_____

_____

_____

b. How should those within the church respond to their spiritual leaders (1 Thessalonians 5:12–13)?

_____

_____

_____

2. Many Christians forsake their God-given responsibility to edify other believers (including their spiritual leaders), and others act as if God has appointed them to be a "God-cop" in the church. In 1 Thessalonians 5:13 Paul presents one of the most powerful verses in the Bible on how to minister effectively to other believers. Please draw a line from the individual problem to the appropriate ministry response *without looking at your Bible.*

a. **Unruly** (NIV: "idle and disruptive")	**uphold them** (NIV: "help them")
b. **Fainthearted** (NIV: "disheartened")	**warn them**
c. **Weak**	**comfort them** (NIV: "encourage them")

3. a. If you are a Christian, has another believer ever warned you when you needed encouragement (the "God-cop" syndrome), encouraged you to continue in sin

(the "sentimental sympathizer" syndrome), or failed to uphold you during a time of weakness? What did you learn from that situation?

_____

_____

_____

Would you like to learn how to prepare a life-changing Bible study using a simple 4-step process? Contact Lamplighters and ask about ST-A-R-T.

ADDITIONAL INSIGHTS

b. If you are a Christian, have you ever comforted another believer who needed to be warned, or warned someone who needed to be comforted? How does gaining a better understanding of 1 Thessalonians 5:13 help you minister more effectively to others?

_____

_____

_____

_____

4. List two additional commands that all believers have in their relations with other people (1 Thessalonians 5:15).

1. _____

_____

2. _____

_____

5. a. How can a Christian fulfill God's command to **Rejoice always** (NIV 1984: "Be joyful always") (1 Thessalonians 5:16) when there is so much sin, pain, and injustice in this world?

_____

_____

_____

_____

47

b. What do you think a believer must do (think, remember, etc.) to accomplish God's command and be the witness the Lord intended him or her to be?

_____

_____

_____

_____

6. 1 Thessalonians 5:18 says Christians are to give thanks for everything that happens because it is **the will of God in Christ Jesus for you.** Many believers are confused by this verse because they think it indicates God is the author of the sin that He allows to come into their lives. And if this is true, then God is unrighteous and thereby disqualified to be our righteous redeemer.

a. How did the Old Testament patriarch Joseph understand the relationship between man's sin (his brothers attempt to kill him and then they sold him into slavery) and God's will for his life (Genesis 45:1–8; 50:15–20)?

_____

_____

_____

_____

_____

b. What did the apostle Peter tell the Jews about the relationship between their sin and the sovereign will of God (Acts 2:22–24)?

_____

_____

_____

_____

7. Martin Luther, whose life was continually sought by the established church at the time, said, "I am immortal until God calls me home to heaven." Luther had arrived at a place of faith where he realized that a sovereign God would not allow sinful man to do anything that was not within His permissive will. If you are a Christian, have you come to that place of faith where you trust God explicitly and do not live in (any) fear, so you can give thanks in all things because **this is the will of God in Christ Jesus for you**?

Having trouble with your group? A Lamplighters trainer can help you solve the problem.

ADDITIONAL INSIGHTS

_____

What do you need to do to trust God in all things?

_____

_____

_____

8. a. What do you think it means to **not quench the Spirit** (1 Thessalonians 5:19; NIV 1984: "Do not put out the Spirit's fire")?

_____

_____

_____

b. What do you think a believer must do to be certain that he or she does not **despise prophecies** (1 Thessalonians 5:20)?

_____

_____

_____

_____

_____

c. How can you **test all things** (1 Thessalonians 5:21; 2 Corinthians 10:4–5)?

_____

_____

_____

9. The Bible says to **abstain from every form of evil** (1 Thessalonians 5:22; NIV 1984: "avoid every kind of evil"). This brief statement commands all believers to refrain from doing everything that directly violates God's Word, defiles body, soul, and spirit, and diminishes the believer's witness for Christ to the unsaved world. What things are there in your life that violate God's Word—things that you need to repent of and abstain from?

_____

_____

_____

10. Sometimes believers rationalize their sinful habits, saying that they are "living under grace", or the things they are doing do not harm anyone. When we live unrighteous lives, we are a stumbling block to the unsaved and other believers. The apostle Paul, writing to the Corinthians, refuted the error of justifying sin by redefining it as grace (1 Corinthians 5:1–6). Paul also addressed the topic of "questionable" areas in the Christian life—areas that are not expressly prohibited by Scripture but hinder our spiritual growth and witness for Christ. The Bible is careful to not mention endless lists of specifics (which often leads to legalism), but it does offer guiding principles that should govern a Christian's choices. Look closely at 1 Corinthians 6:12 and 1 Corinthians 10:22. Identify the spiritual principles that should govern every Christian's conduct and then put them in the form of a question that you can ask yourself when you are faced with a decision. As an example the first question may be: *"Even*

though I have the right to do _____, will it be helpful to me and others in the future?" (1 Corinthians 6:12).

1. _____

   _____

2. _____

   _____

3. _____

   _____

4. _____

   _____

11. The apostle Paul concludes 1 Thessalonians with a beautiful prayer on behalf of the young Thessalonian believers. What is God's desire (voiced through Paul's words) for them and all believers, including you (1 Thessalonians 5:23)?

    _____

    _____

    _____

ADDITIONAL INSIGHTS

SEVEN

WORTHY OF GOD'S CALLING

Read 2 Thessalonians 1; other references as given.

Martin Luther said, "A church is like a tender plant. It needs your constant care." Wherever God is at work in and through a local body of believers, the devil is also at work stirring up trouble. Wise are the spiritual leaders and church who are prayerful and watchful over God's flock.

Shortly after Paul penned his first letter to the Thessalonians, seeds of false doctrine began to sprout in the church. Paul's teaching on the day of the Lord (1 Thessalonians 4:13–5:11) was misinterpreted to mean that the church had already entered this terrible future period.

Paul wrote 2 Thessalonians to assure the Thessalonians that God would repay those who persecuted them (chapter 1), to correct their false understanding regarding the day of the Lord (chapter 2), and to exhort the church toward righteous living (chapter 3).

Before you begin, ask God to reveal Himself through His Word and transform you into the image of His Son.

Is your study going well? Consider starting a new group. To learn how, go to www. Lamplighters USA.org/training.

ADD GROUP INSIGHTS BELOW

1. The apostle said the Thessalonian church was **in God our Father and the Lord Jesus Christ** (2 Thessalonians 1:1). What do you think this means?

The two are one

_____
_____
_____

2. Every genuine believer is **in God and the Lord Jesus Christ**. Many Christian churches and denominations, however, were pillars of orthodox evangelicalism, but now have become bastions of religious liberalism. What do you think evangelical Christian churches, ministries, and schools must do to protect themselves against the natural tendency to fall into progressive liberalism?

stay with the inherant,
ward of God
_____
_____

3. The word **peace** has multiple meanings in the Bible. In 2 Thessalonians 1:2, the apostle Paul offers a standard New Testament greeting and wants the Thessalonians to experience the peace that God makes available to all believers who trust Him during the affairs of daily living. Examine the following verses, and give a brief definition of the additional uses of this important word.

a. Ecclesiastes 3:8: _Guard your thoughts and mind_

b. Psalm 119:165: _depend on the scripture_

c. Romans 5:1–2: _access to faith through Jesus Christ_

d. Romans 15:33: _peace through God_

e. Galatians 5:22–23: _fruit of the Spirit love joy peace patience kindness_

f. Ephesians 2:14–17: _access to the Father through one spirit_

It's time to choose your next study. Turn to the back of the study guide for a list of available studies or go online for the latest studies.

g. 2 Corinthians 13:11; 1 Thessalonians 5:13: _love one another_

ADDITIONAL INSIGHTS

4. In 1 Thessalonians 1:3 Paul commended the young Thessalonian believers for their faith, love, and hope. For what did Paul commend them in 2 Thessalonians 1:3?

   Faith love Hope

5. Spiritual growth (also known as progressive sanctification) in the believer's life is not a mysterious process. From the following verses identify several key elements that must be present for a Christian's spiritual growth to flourish.

   a. Romans 10:17: _hearing the word of God_

   b. Ephesians 4:11–14: _maturity_

   c. Ephesians 4:15–17: _speak the truth_

   d. Hebrews 4:2: _Combine the Word with faith_

   e. Hebrews 5:12–14: _faith to destinguish good from evil_

55

f. Hebrews 10:24-25: _encourage one another_

g. Isaiah 55:6-8: _seek the Lord_

6. a. Besides growing in faith and love, what other evidences of spiritual growth was Paul pleased to see in the lives of the Thessalonian believers (2 Thessalonians 1:4)?

b. The young Thessalonian church was undergoing both **persecutions and tribulations** (2 Thessalonians 1:4). What is the difference between these two terms?

c. When did God promise the Thessalonians relief from their persecutions and tribulations (2 Thessalonians 1:7)?

they became a model to believers

7. The Thessalonians' patient and faithful response to their persecutions and tribulations indicated that God was rightly preparing them for a glorious entrance into His kingdom (2 Thessalonians 1:5). In other words, God was sovereignly selecting the trials, including their severity, that came into their lives, and He was providing sufficient grace to overcome every trial. Doesn't that give you a different perspective on trials?

a. How else will God's righteous judgment be manifested and when will it occur (2 Thessalonians 1:6–8)?

_____

_____

_____

It's a good time to begin praying and inviting new people for your next Open House.

ADDITIONAL
INSIGHTS

b. How does the Bible describe God's judgment of the unsaved (2 Thessalonians 1:8–9)?

_____

_____

c. What will be the response of those who are saved (His saints) when Christ comes (2 Thessalonians 1:7, 10)?

_____

_____

8. The certainty of Christ's return and the awesome reality of God's coming judgment on the unsaved, coupled with the marvel and amazement of believers seeing the resurrected Christ for the first time, led Paul to pray continually for the spiritual advancement of the Thessalonian believers (2 Thessalonians 1:11–12).

a. What three things did Paul pray for the Thessalonian believers (2 Thessalonians 1:11)?

_____

_____

b. What was the ultimate goal of Paul's prayer for their spiritual growth (2 Thessalonians 1:12)?

_____

_____

c. What must be both present and active in a believer's life for this perfect union and unity between God and man to exist?

_____

_____

9. How can a Christian know for certain that he or she is living by grace and not simply performing religious acts in the power of their own flesh (Galatians 5:16–25)?

_____

_____

_____

_____

_____

EIGHT

COUNTDOWN TO ETERNITY

> ## Read 2 Thessalonians 2;
> ## other references as given.

In 2 Thessalonians 1 the apostle Paul commended the Thessalonian believers for their continued spiritual growth (vs. 3–5), reminded them of God's coming judgment upon the unsaved (vs. 6–9), and reassured them that God would judge those who persecuted them (vs. 6–9). The Thessalonians, suffering for their faith in Christ, would be rewarded for their faithfulness when Christ returned (vs. 10–12).

In chapter 2 Paul addresses a doctrinal error that had crept into the church. The chapter contains theological truths about end times found nowhere else in the Bible—truths that are indispensable to the believer's understanding of the end times.

Before you begin, ask God to reveal Himself through His Word and transform you into the image of His Son.

Many groups study the Final Exam the week after the final lesson for three reasons: (1) someone might come to Christ, (2) believers gain assurance of salvation, (3) group members learn how to share the gospel.

ADD GROUP INSIGHTS BELOW

1. In 2 Thessalonians 2:1 the words **Now, brethren, concerning the coming of our Lord** call Paul's readers to a heightened level of attentiveness and serve to identity the specific topic he's about to address.

   a. What truth did Paul want his readers to consider (2 Thessalonians 2:1)? Please be as accurate as possible with your answer.

   _____

   _____

b. What didn't he want to happen (2 Thessalonians 2:2)?

_____

_____

2. The origin of the false doctrine was unknown at the time of
Paul's letter. Some thought it was the result of a prophecy (a
spirit), and others speculated that it was the result of a verbal
report. Still others believed Paul had written it himself in a
letter. Rather than becoming defensive for being misquoted
or wasting time trying to uncover the source of the wrong
teaching, Paul deliberately directs his readers to the truth.
Truth is always the enemy of error.

a. What three things must happen before the day of the
Lord occurs (2 Thessalonians 2:3–7)?

1. _____

2. _____

3. _____

b. What other names does the Bible use to describe this
future world ruler who exalts himself above everything
that is called God or is worshipped (Matthew 24:15; 1
John 2:18)?

_____

_____

_____

3. The Thessalonians misinterpreted their circumstances
(persecution) and thought they were living in the day of
the Lord. During the early Christian period (AD 33–325) the
church often wrongly believed that they were living in the
end times and several Roman emperors were the Antichrist.
Throughout the history of the church, countless religious
groups have offered wild predictions about the date of
Christ's return and the identity of the Antichrist. The goal of

studying the end times is not to build calendars but to build *confidence* in Jesus' return and *conviction* to reach the lost for Christ. What biblical truths should all Christians remember so they aren't deceived by false religious teachers who claim to be the Christ (Matthew 24:4–8, 36; 1 Thessalonians 5:1–3)?

If the leader asks all the study questions, the group discussion will be more likely to stay on track.

ADDITIONAL
INSIGHTS

_____

_____

_____

_____

_____

4. a. What specific things will the Antichrist or man of sin do that will reveal his true identity and nature (2 Thessalonians 2:4, 9–10)?

_____

_____

_____

_____

b. Who or what do you think is restraining the man of sin at this time (2 Thessalonians 2:6–7)?

_____

_____

_____

_____

c. What will eventually happen to the Antichrist, and when will this happen (2 Thessalonians 2:8)?

_____

_____

_____

5. What will happen to those who **did not receive the love of the truth, that they might be saved** (2 Thessalonians 2:10–12)?

_____

_____

_____

_____

6. The apostle Paul reassured the Thessalonian believers that they wouldn't perish in these terrifying end times because God had **chosen** and **called** them for salvation (2 Thessalonians 2:13–14). The words **God from the beginning chose you for salvation** are often disturbing to some Christians, but they don't need to be. If you are a Christian, you had absolutely no ability or strength to save yourself (Isaiah 53:6; Jeremiah 17:9; John 3:19–20; Romans 3:10–12; 2 Corinthians 4:4; Ephesians 2:1–3, 5, 11–12). God chose you; you didn't choose Him! The idea of Christians thinking that they can save themselves is both unscriptural and idolatrous.

a. How does God choose people for salvation (2 Thessalonians 2:13; John 16:7–11; Acts 16:30–31; Titus 3:5)?

_____

_____

_____

_____

b. How does God call people for salvation (2 Thessalonians 2:14)?

_____

_____

7. Some believers are confused about their life purpose. If you are a Christian, why did God save you (2 Thessalonians 2:14)? Please be as accurate with your answer as possible.

_____

_____

_____

_____

It's time to order your next study. Allow enough time to get the books so you can distribute them at the Open House. Consider ordering 2-3 extra books for newcomers.

_____

ADDITIONAL INSIGHTS

8. When right or correct (Bible) doctrine is properly applied to life, it brings about right living. Tyson Edwards said, "Doctrine is the necessary foundation of duty; if the theory is not correct, the practice cannot be right. Tell me what a man believes and I will tell you what he will do."

a. Conversely, wrong doctrine, as some of the Thessalonians had adopted, had produced wrong living (2 Thessalonians 3:11–12). What did the apostle Paul want the Thessalonians to do with the teachings (traditions) he taught them (2 Thessalonians 2:15)?

_____

_____

_____

_____

_____

b. What evidence do you see in your life that you hold solidly to the Bible teachings you have been taught from God's Word?

_____

_____

_____

_____

9. a. List three tremendous gifts God has given every one who is redeemed or saved (2 Thessalonians 2:16).

_____

_____

_____

_____

_____

b. What else does God want to do for you if you are a Christian (2 Thessalonians 2:17)?

_____

_____

_____

_____

NINE

LET THE WORD
RUN SWIFTLY

Read 2 Thessalonians 3; other references as given.

In 2 Thessalonians 1 Paul assured the believers that they weren't living in the day of the Lord. Their persecutions, severe as they were, were the world's continual attempt to silence the truth of Christ spoken through the lives of His witnesses.

In 2 Thessalonians 2 Paul corrected the believers' understanding of the day of the Lord. Although the mystery of lawlessness is already at work (2 Thessalonians 2:7), three things must take place before the actual day of the Lord: (1) there must be a time of great rebellion or falling away from the truth (2 Thessalonians 2:3), (2) the man of sin must be revealed (2 Thessalonians 2:3–4) and (3) the restrainer must be removed (2 Thessalonians 2:6–7).

In chapter 3 the apostle addresses several practical aspects of Christian living. Believers should be working for Christ, not waiting idly for His return. Jesus said, **Do you not say, "There are still four months and then comes the harvest"? Behold, I say to you, lift up your eyes and look at the fields, for they are already white for harvest!** (John 4:35).

Before you begin, ask God to reveal Himself through His Word and transform you into the image of His Son.

Final Exam:

Are you meeting next week to study the Final Exam? To learn how to present it effectively, contact Lamplighters.

————

ADD GROUP
INSIGHTS BELOW

1. What three things did Paul ask the Thessalonian believers to pray on his behalf (2 Thessalonians 3:1–2)?

   1. _____

2. _____

3. _____

2. Do you pray that the **word of the Lord would run swiftly** (NIV: "spread rapidly") throughout the world? If not, would you do so right now? Would you ask God now to use you to spread His message of truth?

_____

_____

_____

_____

3　a. What do you think it means for the word of the Lord to be **glorified** (NIV: "honored") in the life of a believer?

_____

_____

_____

b. If you are a Christian, in what areas of your life could you glorify or honor the word of the Lord to a greater extent?

_____

_____

_____

4. Paul wanted the word of the Lord to spread rapidly, just as it had been doing through the Thessalonians (2 Thessalonians 3:1). Obviously the young Thessalonian believers had been a spiritual encouragement to the apostle. What specific things could you do to encourage and inspire other believers, especially in relation to the spread of the gospel?

_____

_____

_____

5. Sometimes God's people are afraid to take bold steps of faith such as glorifying or honoring the word of God and renouncing sin in their lives. Perhaps they're fearful of falling back into sin and dishonoring the Lord. What twofold promise does the Bible give every believer who wants to glorify or honor the word of the Lord more fully in his life (2 Thessalonians 3:3)?

_____

_____

_____

Would you like to learn how to lead someone through this same study? It's not hard. Go to www.Lamplighters USA.org to register for *free* online leadership training.

ADDITIONAL INSIGHTS

6. In 2 Thessalonians 3:6 Paul addressed a specific problem in the church that had developed as a result of the Thessalonians' faulty understanding of the day of the Lord. Some within the church, convinced that they were living in the day of the Lord, had stopped working (2 Thessalonians 3:6, 11). The apostle had addressed this problem previously (1 Thessalonians 4:11–12), but apparently some were persisting in their sin.

   a. How did the apostle Paul describe the conduct of these individuals (2 Thessalonians 3:6–7, 11)?

   _____

   _____

   _____

   b. How did the conduct of those who would not work affect the rest of the church (2 Thessalonians 3:8)?

   _____

   _____

   c. How did Paul's work ethic differ from those who weren't working and who were waiting idly for Christ's return and the day of the Lord (2 Thessalonians 3:7–8)?

   _____

_____

_____

d. Now honestly evaluate your work ethic. Are your effort, attitude, and commitment to excellence (remember, we are to "excel still more"; 1 Thessalonians 4:1 NASB) a good witness for Christ?

Yes / No

If not, perhaps you should consider asking God and your employer for forgiveness and ask God to help you be a better worker.

7. a. What did Paul command the Thessalonian believers to do to restore those who were sinning (2 Thessalonians 3:6, 14)?

_____

_____

_____

_____

b. What important truth did Paul admonish the church to remember when they dealt with those who would not work and were acting like busybodies in the church (2 Thessalonians 3:14–15)?

_____

_____

_____

_____

8. The goal of confronting another believer who is living in sin is spiritual restoration. Unfortunately some Christians are unwilling to accept their biblical responsibility to confront another believer whose life is a reproach to God and a poor reflection on Christ. Other believers accept their biblical

responsibility but fail to follow the biblical plan of speaking the truth in love (Ephesians 4:15).

a. What should every Christian do *before* he or she talks with another believer who is living in sin (Galatians 6:1)?

_____

_____

_____

_____

b. What is the prescribed biblical procedure for talking with a sinning brother or sister (Matthew 18:15–18)?

_____

_____

_____

_____

_____

9. We have now come to the end of our study on 1 and 2 Thessalonians. The Bible says, **the word...did not profit them, not being mixed with faith in them that heard** (Hebrews 4:2 KJV). List at least three truths you learned in your study of 1 and 2 Thessalonians that will change your life forever.

1. _____

_____

2. _____

_____

3. _____

_____

• • • •

Congratulations:

You have just completed a challenging study of Paul's two letters to the Thessalonians. Perhaps you were inspired by the Thessalonian believers' bold reception of the word of God and how they turned from their idols to become powerful witnesses for Christ. Now is the time for all of us who profess Christ as Savior and Lord to do the same: to accept God's word—**not as the word of men, but as it is in truth, the word of God**—and live God-honoring lives. (1 Thessalonians 2:13).

LEADER'S GUIDE

Lesson 1: The Life-Changing Word

1. a. Paul received a vision from God of a man from Macedonia who pleaded with the apostle to help his fellow Macedonians (Acts 16:9–10).

   b. Only Paul received the vision, but he shared the vision with others (Silas [Acts 15:40], Timothy [Acts 16:3–4), and Luke [Acts 16:10, "we"]) and sought their counsel. Paul fulfilled the biblical principle of seeking wise counsel (Proverbs 1:5). Paul acted wisely by seeking and listening to godly counsel (Proverbs 12:15), and a wise plan was established (Proverbs 20:18). Notice the combined aspects of God's revelation and sanctified human reason ("we concluded") were both to discern God's will for their lives.

2. a. Paul was grateful for the faith, love, and hope that were being manifested in their lives. Answers will vary.

   b. 1. Believers must be diligent to trust (believe) God's promises during the temptations to doubt, lies that undermine faith, and the spiritual attacks from others who do not believe. In this sense faith is a work. 2. True love (Christlike love) sacrifices and labors for the physical, emotional, and spiritual advancement and salvation of others. 3. The believer's hope in God and His promises should be steadfast so he can, without wavering, be the recipient of God's promises and live with a heavenly confidence.

3. Answers will vary.

4. a. God's power was manifested in and through the apostle Paul's preaching because his life was clean from sin and he was dedicated to God's purposes.

   b. The Holy Spirit brought deep conviction upon the Thessalonians.

   c. Paul's preaching was presented as life-changing truth from God that he had embraced, not theoretical musings about spiritual speculations or man-made religious traditions.

5. a. Paul said he was not ashamed of the gospel of Jesus Christ because

it possessed God's power to save everyone who believed. It did not matter if they were Jews or Gentiles. The gospel of Jesus Christ would save them. For this reason, Paul was not ashamed to proclaim it.

b. Paul wanted the Corinthians to have a faith that rested solely on the truth of the gospel of Jesus Christ (1 Corinthians 2:5). He didn't want his listeners to accept the message he preached because of any perceived (human) wisdom or eloquence (1 Corinthians 2:4). In fact, said Paul, he originally preached the gospel to the Corinthians when he was emotionally drained and fearful (1 Corinthians 2:3). Notice that Paul had determined beforehand how he would preach the gospel to the Corinthians (1 Corinthians 2:2). He wanted Christ, not himself or his preaching, to be the object of their faith.

6. a. Answers will vary. Perhaps many preachers don't think the people want to hear the Bible. Perhaps they don't feel they have adequate theological training and don't want to tell others something that is incorrect. Perhaps they are afraid that people will leave the church if they preach the truth.

b. 1. Man-made religious traditions (Mark 7:5–8).
2. The Old Testament Law of Moses as obligatory for New Testament Christians (1 Timothy 1:3–8).
3. Religious myths and fables (2 Timothy 4:4). These are religious speculations that have no way of being substantiated or refuted.
4. Fables (2 Peter 1:16). The Greek word (*muthos*) is used for mythical stories about gods, the creation of the world, and miraculous happenings. The same Greek word is used in 2 Timothy 4:4.

c. Pray for those who are proclaiming God's Word, especially for God to give them spiritual courage to proclaim the gospel with boldness.

7. a. 1. They were following the Lord as had been taught them by the apostle Paul even though they were experiencing persecution (v. 6).
2. They were experiencing Holy Spirit–inspired joy during their trials (v. 6).
3. Their Christian witness was so exemplary that other believers attempted to emulate them (v. 7).
4. Their faith was a powerful encouragement to believers in other areas of Greece (v. 8).

b. 1. They received or welcomed those who proclaimed the Word of

God (v. 9). 2. They turned from idols to serve the living and true God (v. 9). 3. They eagerly waited for and anticipated the return of Jesus Christ (v. 10).

8. Answers will vary.

9. Paul wanted the Corinthians to examine or test themselves to determine if they were saved or born again. Note that Paul never said he thought or said they were unsaved. He simply encouraged them to test themselves to determine if they were genuinely saved.

10. a. 1. A genuine Christian keeps or obeys God's commandments (1 John 2:3). 2. A genuine Christian doesn't continue in habitual sin (1 John 3:9). 3. A genuine Christian loves other believers (1 John 3:14). 4. A genuine Christian believes that Jesus is the Christ (1 John 5:1). 5. A genuine Christian can overcome the temptation of this world because of his faith in God (1 John 5:4).
    b. Answers will vary.

Lesson 2: Shepherd's Heart

1. a. The persecution they received at Philippi did not deter the missionaries. They continued to preach the gospel with boldness.
   b. The apostles Peter and John were not intimidated by the threats from the Jewish authorities. Peter and John said they could not stop speaking about the things they had seen (when they walked with Jesus) and heard (what He said).
   c. Answers will vary.

2. When a believer fears man (what he thinks), it's like he is caught in a snare (Proverbs 29:25). Just as a snare prevents an animal from continuing his journey, a believer hinders his spiritual progress. If a believer fears man, he will not be able to be an effective servant of God (Galatians 1:10).

3. a. 1. Paul did not preach the Word incorrectly (with error) (v. 3). 2. He didn't have impure motives when he preached (v. 3). 3. He didn't try to deceive them (v. 3). 4. He didn't use flattery (v. 5). 5. His preaching was not covertly or secretly covetous (v. 5).

b. 1. Paul loved them (v. 8). 2. He preached the truth (gospel) (v. 8). 3. He opened his heart and life to them (v. 8). 4. He worked day and night (assumedly as a tentmaker) so he could provide for his own needs and not be a burden on the young church (v. 9). 5. He lived a holy life before them that authenticated the message he preached (v. 10). 6. He lived righteously before them (v. 10). 7. He maintained a good testimony (**blamelessly**) so he would not cause the young believers to stumble over him (v. 10).

4. Christians should be bold in their proclamation of the gospel to the lost, but they should be gentle, gracious in their demeanor. Paul said he was bold to preach the gospel, but he was gentle with the young believers at Thessalonica. This does not mean that we don't need to be gentle with the unsaved. We should always seek to reflect Christ, who was meek and gentle.

5. 1. Paul understood that God had given him a trust (the gospel), and he was to be responsible and accountable to God for it (1 Thessalonians 2:4). He also realized that God had called him (**approved by God**) to be His servant.

   2. Paul recognized that the truth God had revealed to him was the very Word of God (1 Thessalonians 2:13).

6. a. Approved (v. 4), entrusted (v. 4), not pleasing men (v. 4), but (pleasing) God (v. 4), (God) tests our hearts (v. 4). God is witness (v. 5). Nor do we seek glory from man (v. 6). Laboring day and night (v. 9). You are witnesses (v. 10). (God) is witness (v. 10).

   b. Answers will vary.

7. a. All believers are supposed to live in a manner that represents Christ well. They should not seek their own interests, but rather seek to do the things that bring glory to God.

   b. 1. Believers are to walk (live) worthy of the Lord (Ephesians 4:1). 2. Believers are to walk (live) no longer like the unsaved (Gentiles) (Ephesians 4:17). 3. Believers are to walk in love (Ephesians 5:2). Believers are to walk in the light, which means to live per God's word (Ephesians 5:8). Believers are to walk circumspectly. This means they are to be careful how they conduct their lives (Ephesians 5:15).

8. Paul was very thankful for the way the young Thessalonian believers received the truth.

9. a. The Thessalonians accepted the revelation God gave them through the apostle Paul as the very word of God.

   b. 1. Because the Thessalonians accepted the word of God as the truth, they become imitators of the churches in Judea (1 Thessalonians 2:14). 2. They became true followers of Jesus Christ by following Paul's example of Christian living (1 Thessalonians 1:6). 3. They continued to follow the Lord even though they were being persecuted, and they experienced Holy Spirit–induced joy in the midst of their struggles (1 Thessalonians 1:6). 4. They turned from their idols and served the Lord (1 Thessalonians 1:9).

   c. **The Scripture cannot be broken.** Jesus powerfully affirms the inerrancy and absolute reliability of the Scriptures.

   d. Answers will vary.

10. The Judean churches and the Thessalonian church faced persecution shortly after they came to faith in Christ. Both churches trusted God in the midst of their persecutions and continued to advance the gospel.

11. Satan can hinder or impede God's people, but he doesn't possess the power to stop them permanently. The Greek word (*enkopto*) was originally used of the breaking up of a road to render it impassable, and it was also used of making a break in enemy lines. Later it was used in an athletic sense of cutting in on a runner in a race. Satan has the power to hinder believers, but he doesn't possess the power to stop them permanently from accomplishing God's will for our lives.

12. Answers will vary.

Lesson 3: Established in the Faith

1. a. Paul could no longer endure not knowing how the young Thessalonian believers were doing. He longed to know if they were continuing to grow in the Lord and were being faithful to Christ.

   b. Paul sent Timothy to Thessalonica to help the young believers become more established in the faith (1 Thessalonians 3:2).

2. Paul didn't want to preach the word and then move on. He desperately longed for the Thessalonians to be firmly established in the truth. This reveals Paul's great love for fellow believers and for their spiritual advancement. This verse also reveals Timothy's great love for the Thessalonians and his willingness to risk his safety to serve Paul and to minister to the Thessalonians.

3. a. Paul didn't want the Thessalonians' faith to be shaken when they heard that he (Paul) was continuing to suffer persecution (1 Thessalonians 3:3–4). Paul reminded them that he had told them that the persecutions were probably going to continue.
   b. Persecution is viewed as light and momentary in relation to the weight of eternal glory that the believer will receive in eternity (2 Corinthians 4:17).
   c. Believers must look to God and eternity during their time of trial. They must realize the persecutions they are experiencing will pass away.

4. Paul was concerned that Satan had deceived them and his missionary work would be wasted.

5. 1. Paul was pleased to learn that the Thessalonians were continuing to live by faith. 2. He was pleased to know that they were continuing to love one another. 3. Paul was pleased to learn that they were continuing to think well of him.

6. a. Although the apostle Paul lived his life in the fullness of the Holy Spirit and experienced the joy of walking with God, he was so concerned with the spiritual wellbeing of other believers that he could honestly say that he "really lived" when they were living fully for God. This statement demonstrates the intense desire Paul had for the spiritual growth of other Christians and is an example for all believers to follow in their relationship to other Christians.
   b. To stand fast or stand firm in the Lord means a Christian is wholeheartedly committed to following Christ and is unmoved by affliction and persecution and unshaken by Christ's detractors.

7. Answers will vary.

8. Answers will vary.

9. Faith comes by hearing and receiving God's Word (Romans 10:17).

10. a. Paul asked God to make a way for him to visit the Thessalonians (v. 11). He also prayed that the Lord would increase their love for one another and for all people (v. 12).
    b. The Thessalonians would stand before God blameless and holy (vs. 12–13).

11. a. Answers will vary.
    b. Answers will vary.

Lesson 4: Excel in Christ

1. Paul told the Thessalonians to continue to grow in Christ (**abound more and more**). The New American Standard Bible says they were to "excel still more." All Christians should abound or excel in their relationship with Christ.

2. a. Answers will vary.
   b. Answers will vary.

3. Answers will vary.

4. a. It's God's will for all believers to be sanctified (set apart for God) in the area of moral purity (1 Thessalonians 4:3). Christians should abstain from all forms of sexual immorality (1 Thessalonians 4:3). The institution of marriage and the (marriage) bed should not be defiled by sexual immorality (Hebrews 13:4). God will judge those who fornicate and those who commit adultery. The explosion of sexually transmitted diseases among those who engage in free sex is perhaps an example of God's judgment. However, not everyone who has a sexually transmitted disease has been immoral.
   b. Adultery is sexual intercourse between a married man with someone other than his wife, or between a married woman and someone other than her husband. It is distinguished from fornication, which is sexual intercourse by an unmarried person.

5. a. 1. Simple/naive (v. 7). 2. Someone void of understanding (v. 7). 3. As an ox to the slaughter (v. 22). 4. As a bird about to fly into a snare (v. 23).
   b. 1. It is God's will (1 Thessalonians 4:3). 2. Believers are not to live their lives driven by passion, like the unsaved who don't know God (1 Thessalonians 4:5). 3. When a believer engages in sexual sin, he is defrauding the other person (1 Thessalonians 4:6). 4. God will judge the believer who is sexually immoral (1 Thessalonians 4:6).

6. a. Matthew 6:13: Pray for God to keep you away from situations (people and places) that would lead you into temptation.
   b. 1 John 1:8; 2:2: Call sin, sin (1 John 1:8, 9). Don't rationalize, justify, or rename it. Realize, as believers, you have forgiveness in Jesus Christ.
   c. James 1:12–16: Recognize that sin is the culmination of a series of steps or events which lead to sin (unsanctified areas in our lives leave us open to temptation, which entices us to be drawn away by evil, which leads to sin).
   d. James 5:16: Believers need to find someone to confess sin to who will pray effectively for strength to overcome temptation.
   e. Proverbs 5:20–21: Believers need to realize that God sees everything. There is no such thing as a secret sexual sin. It may be hidden from others, but not from God.
   f. 1 Corinthians 10:13: God will never allow you to be tempted by sexual sin without giving you the way (through Christ) to overcome the sin and the temptation to sin.
   g. 2 Corinthians 10:4–5: Believers need to memorize Scripture so they are able to bring every thought captive to Christ (God's will, which is sexual purity among other things).
   h. Philippians 4:8: Believers are commanded to focus their minds on things that are pure and honorable, not the things that lead to sexual sin (lust, etc.).
   i. John 8:3–11: Believers need to believe sexual sin can be overcome. Jesus told the woman caught in adultery to "go and sin no more." Notice that Jesus called her conduct sin. He did not whitewash it. Jesus essentially said, "Stop it right now." While this may sound simplistic, those caught in sexual sin need to know that they can overcome their struggle through Christ. That's the power of the cross!
   j. Matthew 5:27–28: Believers must know that lust (the volitional choice to mentally conceive a sexual encounter with another person) violates

God's standard of sexual purity. Jesus said lust constitutes committing adultery in the heart. While this is strong language, and lusting is an obvious violation of God's standard of moral purity, lust is not the same as the physical act of adultery.

7. The Holy Spirit resides in every believer, and He guides us into the truth through promptings to do right, uneasiness when we are tempted to sin, and a lack of peace when we are about to make decisions that are contrary to God's will (John 16:13). As believers mature in Christ and continue to gain a better knowledge of God's Word, they are able more strongly to sense God's leading through the internal ministry of the Holy Spirit (1 John 2:26–27).

8. The Thessalonian believers were already being a powerful witness for Christ to others at Thessalonica and throughout other parts of Greece. Now Paul was commanding them to make sure their personal lives authenticated the message. As young believers they were undoubtedly enthusiastic about spreading the gospel, but they needed to make sure their personal testimonies also reflected Christ so that the message of Christ would not be discredited.

9. a. God didn't want the Thessalonians to be ignorant of what happens to those who have died in Christ. While believers often sorrow for those who have died in Christ, they don't sorrow like the unsaved, who have no hope of seeing their loved ones again.

   b. The resurrection of those who have died in Christ should bring hope and comfort to all believers.

   c. When Christ returns for His saints, He will descend with a shout and the voice of an archangel and with the trumpet (sound) of God. (1 Thessalonians 4:16). Those believers who have already died will be resurrected before those are living. Then those believers who are still alive when Christ returns will be caught up or raptured to meet the Lord in the air. From that time forward we shall be always with the Lord (1 Thessalonians 4:17).

10. Answers will vary.

Lesson 5: Day of the Lord

1. The day of the Lord will come suddenly and without warning, the way a thief comes in the night. It is important not to press this illustration too far to mean that Christ will come at night, even though it will be night in some parts of the world when He comes.

2. a. Isaiah 13:9–13: Cruel, wrath, fierce anger, desolation, destruction of sinners (v. 9). Stars of heaven and constellations will not give light, sun and moon will be darkened (v. 10). Punish the world for its evil and the world for its iniquity, the arrogance of the proud will be halted, the haughtiness of the terrible will be laid low (v. 11). Mortal men will be rare (this signifies the number of deaths during this time) (v. 12). The heavens will be shaken, and the earth will be moved out of its place in the day of God's fierce anger (v. 13).

   b. Joel 2:28–32: God's Spirit will be poured out on all flesh, and sons and daughters shall prophesy, old men will dream dreams, and your young men shall see visions (v. 28). God will pour out His Spirit in those days on His menservants and maidservants (vs. 28–29). God will show wonders (blood, fire, pillars of smoke, sun turning to darkness, moon the color of blood) before the coming of the great and awesome day of the Lord (vs. 30–31). A time when some will still come to salvation (v. 32).

   c. Amos 5:18: A time (day) of darkness and not light (v. 18). It will be a day of escaping one danger and running into another (flee from a lion and meet a bear, escaping into a house only to be bitten by a serpent).

   d. 2 Peter 3:10: A time that will come suddenly upon the world (like a thief in the night), the heavens will pass away with a great noise, the elements will melt away because of fervent heat, the earth and the works on it will be burned up.

3. Like birth pangs upon a woman, the day of the Lord (1) will come suddenly, (2) will become progressively more intense, and (3) will be inescapable.

4. 1. There will be many false teachers claiming to be the Christ (Matthew 24:4–5), and false prophets will deceive many (Matthew 24:11).

   2. There will continue to be wars, famines, pestilences, earthquakes (Matthew 24:6–7).

3. Christians will be persecuted (Matthew 24:9).

4. Lawlessness will abound and people will become self-seeking and self-preserving (**the love of many will grow cold**; Matthew 24:12).

5. God delivers believers from the wrath to come (1 Thessalonians 1:10) and 1 Thessalonians 5:9 says God has not appointed us to wrath, but to obtain salvation through our Lord Jesus Christ.

6. a. Believers should walk in the light of God, being watchful (discerning), and sober (spiritually alert) (1 Thessalonians 5:5–6). Believers should also put on the **breastplate of faith and love** and allow their minds to be protected by the constant hope and assurance of God's promise of salvation (1 Thessalonians 5:8). Knowing the coming terror of the Lord when God unleashes His wrath upon a sinful world, believers should seek to reach the lost with the gospel of Jesus Christ before it is too late (2 Corinthians 5:11).

   b. Answers will vary.

7. An ancient breastplate protected the very center of a warrior's being. In the same way, a Christian is a spiritual warrior for God who must protect his innermost being from the attacks (lies, doubts, slander, gossip, fears, etc.) that will inevitably come and seek to destroy him or her. Believers must put on the breastplate of faith (knowing and believing God's Word) and love (seeing all things from the perspective of an infinitely loving God who wants His followers to represent that love to others).

8. There are two possible interpretations. 1. The first interpretation means that whether we die in Christ (sleep) or are alive when He returns, we belong to Christ. 2. The second interpretation indicates that whether we are spiritually lethargic/apathetic (sleep) or spiritually alert (awake), we will be preserved and redeemed by the Lord. Since the apostle Paul just explained the resurrection of the dead in Christ in detail (1 Thessalonians 4:13–18) and the immediate context presents the possibility of a Christian being apathetic, the second interpretation seems to be the better choice. If this is correct, then this verse provides strong support for the doctrine of the eternal security of the believer.

9. a. 1. Knowing that God will not allow believers to experience the wrath

of God should be a great comfort.

    2. Knowing that all believers will eventually be reunited should be a great comfort.

    3. Knowing that there will be a day when God will finally judge sin is a great comfort to believers.

b. Believers should do everything they can to represent Christ well so that others might come to salvation in Christ. The apostle Paul said that he would do all things (possible) so that others might be saved (1 Corinthians 9:22–23). Believers should share the gospel every time they can to help the unsaved understand the message of salvation and be redeemed.

c. Answers will vary.

10. Answers will vary, but could include the following: Besides somewhat similar moral codes, which could be expected, what other similarities have you observed? Chances are they are simply parroting something they have heard someone say, and they do not have an answer. If this happens, perhaps you could say, "You know, I actually see more differences than similarities." If you sense an opportunity to continue, you could name one or two. Note: It may be a good idea to purchase a chart that compares the major religions so you could offer a couple of examples.

Lesson 6: Harmony in God's Family

1. a. (1) Spiritual leaders have been called to work (labor among you) (1 Thessalonians 5:12–13). It is called **a good work** in 1 Timothy 3:1. A good, spiritual leader should work hard studying God's Word, praying, and ministering to the people God has entrusted to His care. A lazy shepherd is a charlatan who neither understands his calling (if he ever had one) or the spiritual needs of the people. (2) Spiritual leaders should have the spiritual courage to preach and teach the truth, including admonishing people to greater commitment to the Lord (1 Thessalonians 5:12). (3) Spiritual leaders must lead (**and are over you**) (1 Thessalonians 5:12). A good spiritual leader is not a pollster who simply surveys the wishes of the people, promotes cooperation, and navigates the safest position. A good spiritual leader leads under God's leading (**over you in the Lord**).

b. They should esteem or honor them very highly in love for their work's sake. They should also seek to live at peace with others in the family of God.

2. a. Unruly .... warn them
   b. Fainthearted .... comfort them
   c. Weak .... uphold them

3. a. Answers will vary.
   b. Answers will vary.

4. 1. Don't repay evil with evil. Notice that any form of revenge is called evil.
   2. Pursue what is good for everyone, including yourself. This does not mean that you give others whatever they want or demand. The word *good* here is used in a God-centered way.

5. a. A Christian must have a firm grasp on the sovereignty of God. The believer must understand that God is too good to be unkind, too wise to make mistakes, and too powerful to be overcome with evil. If he can see this, he will, over time, be able to see all things working together for good to those who love God and those who are called according to His purpose (Romans 8:28). By faith, a believer can learn how to rejoice always, knowing that a sovereign God will not allow anything to come into his or her life without allowing it for His glory and the spiritual good of the individual.
   b. Answers will vary.

6. a. Genesis 45:1–8. Joseph believed God had sent him to Egypt before his family to preserve their lives (Genesis 45:5). He was able to see God's sovereign hand without denying their sin (*you sold me*). In this passage there is no hint of condemning his brothers because he saw God accomplishing His perfect will even though man (his brothers) acted sinfully.

   Genesis 50:15–20. At the death of Jacob's (Joseph's father), Joseph's brothers still worried that he would do evil to them (Genesis 50:15–17). Rather than accepting Joseph at his word, they lied to him, but he assured them that he was not seeking revenge. He reiterated that they had done evil and their original motives were also evil (Genesis 50:20,

you meant evil against me), but he said **God meant it for good.** These are two of the clearest passages in the Bible that show God using, but not excusing, man's sin to accomplish His sovereign will.

b. Peter said Jesus was delivered by the determined purpose and foreknowledge of God into the hands of lawless men (the Jewish leaders, Romans) who crucified Him (Acts 2:22–23). Peter went on to say that God raised Jesus up again because it was impossible for him to be held by death (Acts 2:24).

7. Answers will vary.

8. a. To quench the Holy Spirit means to resist the Spirit's promptings in a believer's life to live wholeheartedly for God, accomplishing His will for His glory.

b. In the early church, false teachers and false prophets were common (Acts 15:1–2; 2 Corinthians 11:13–15; 1 Timothy 1:3–7; 2 Peter 2:1; Jude 3–19). Even though Paul commended the Thessalonians for their commitment to the authority of Scripture (1 Thessalonians 2:13), he wanted to be sure they did not reject all prophetic utterances prior to the completion of New Testament revelation (1 Corinthians 13:8–10).

c. Since Paul had told the Thessalonians not to reject all prophetic utterances, he then instructed them how to do it. They were to test the spirits, which meant to compare what they heard by the revealed word of God. This is equally good advice for believers today.

9. Answers will vary.

10. 1. Even though I have the right to do (_____), will it be helpful to me and others in the future (1 Corinthians 6:12)?
2. Even though I have the right to do (_____), will it eventually lead to bondage or addiction (1 Corinthians 6:12)?
3. Even though I have the right to do (_____), will it edify others and build me up spiritually (1 Corinthians 10:22)?

11. God's desire is for all believers to be sanctified (or set apart) completely and for them to be preserved blameless when Christ returns.

Lesson 7: Worthy of God's Calling

1. To be in God and the Lord Jesus Christ means the individual is redeemed or born again. For the church to be in God and the Lord Jesus Christ means that each individual within the church is regenerated or born again. Paul is saying the Thessalonian believers possessed a clear testimony of salvation by faith in Christ and their lives gave clear evidence of genuine fruit. Every church should make sure that those who claim to be part of the church can give a clear testimony of saving faith in Christ.

2. Answers will vary. Churches, Christian schools and colleges, as well as other Christian ministries should require that all spiritual leaders and workers (and in the case of a church, members) are saved and can provide a clear testimony of salvation by faith in Christ alone. Regarding Christian colleges, universities, and seminaries, students should be required to include a clear Christian testimony upon application.

3. a. Ecclesiastes 3:8: A condition of relative, social tranquility contrasted to a time of war.
   b. Psalm 119:165: A state of inner, spiritual contentment and serenity resulting from a knowledge of God and His word, which produces an emotional strength to overcome personal offenses.
   c. Romans 5:1–2: God's judicial declaration and guarantee of the removal of His righteous hostility (God's wrath) to those who are born again or redeemed.
   d. Romans 15:33: A primary attribute of God.
   e. Galatians 5:22–23: One of the nine-fold fruit(s) of the Holy Spirit.
   f. Ephesians 2:14–17: God is the means of peace and is the One who makes (the source) peace between both people and peoples who cannot make peace between themselves.
   g. 2 Corinthians 13:11; 1 Thessalonians 5:13: God's will and His desired state of harmony and unity that should exist between all believers.

4. Paul commended the Thessalonians for the growth in their faith and the increased love they were expressing to one another.

5. a. Romans 10:17: Christians must have access to the word of God. Faith does not occur without God's truth.

b. Ephesians 4:11–14: Christians must have access to sound, biblical teaching from those called by God.

c. Ephesians 4:15–17: Christians must believe that God wants them to become spiritually mature.

d. Hebrews 4:2: Christians must respond to the word of God in faith.

e. Hebrews 5:12–14: Christians must take some measure of responsibility for their own spiritual progress and realize that it takes time to become spiritually mature.

f. Hebrews 10:24–25: Christians must assume their responsibility to encourage other believers and allow other Christians to encourage them

g. Isaiah 55:6–8: Christians must accept the fact that God's ways are higher than man's ways. The believer must constantly accept what the Bible teaches when it conflicts with his own thinking.

6. a. The Thessalonians were persevering and trusting God in all their persecutions and trials.

b. Persecutions are the difficulties that Christians experience as a result of their devotion to Christ. Tribulations are the difficulties that naturally come as a result of living in a fallen world.

c. Relief would come when Jesus Christ returns in blazing fire with His angels to establish his kingdom (1 Thessalonians 1:7).

7. a. God will repay those who persecuted the Thessalonians (v. 6) and He will punish all those who do not know Him and have not obeyed the gospel of Jesus Christ (v. 8). Here the word *gospel* is used in a wider sense and refers to the teachings of God's Word.

b. Flaming fire, (God's) vengeance, punishment, everlasting destruction, abandonment from God (NIV: "shut out from the presence of the Lord"; v. 9).

c. Believers will be relieved from the persecutions and marvel at Christ when He returns.

8. a. Paul prayed for the Thessalonians to allow God to (1) help them live righteously (worthy of His calling), (2) work in their hearts to bring about every one of His desires for their lives, and (3) enable them to live by faith.

b. For God to be glorified in and through their lives and for them in turn to reflect that glory, according to (or in proportion to) the grace that God extends to them.

   c. God's grace must be received in salvation, and the believer must learn to live by grace.

9. The fruit of the Spirit (love, joy, peace, patience, kindness, goodness, etc.; Galatians 5:22–23) cannot be manufactured by the flesh on a consistent basis. Believers, therefore, can know if they are walking (living) by the power of the Holy Spirit if these nine evidences of the fruit of the Spirit are consistently manifested in their lives.

Lesson 8: Countdown to Eternity

1. a. The return of Jesus Christ
     b. Paul didn't want the Thessalonians to mistakenly believe that the day of the Lord had already come.

2. a. 1. There must be a great falling away from the truth (1 Thessalonians 2:3).
         2. The man of sin (Antichrist) must be revealed (1 Thessalonians 2:3).
         3. The restrainer must be removed (1 Thessalonians 2:7).
     b. 1. Man of sin (2 Thessalonians 2:3), 2. Abomination of Desolation (Matthew 24:15). 3. Antichrist (1 John 2:18).

3. 1. Many false teachers and "prophets" will proclaim themselves to be the Christ (Matthew 24:4–8).
     2. Many of these false teachers will be very persuasive. The phrases *Take heed that no one deceives you* and *will deceive many* highlight the threat of spiritual seduction for Christians.
     3. Since there are already wars, famines, earthquakes, as well as international conflict, there will likely be an increase in these things prior to the day of the Lord (Matthew 24:4–8).
     4. No man knows the exact hour of Christ's return (Matthew 24:36). All who set an exact date for Christ's return are false teachers.
     5. Christians can and should know the signs leading up to Christ's return (1 Thessalonians 5:1–3).
     6. Christ's return will come as a thief in the night (1 Thessalonians 5:1–3). Apparently, there will be a brief time of world peace immediately

prior to Christ's return or perhaps the pronouncement of such (1 Thessalonians 5:1–3).

4. a. 1. He will oppose everything that is truly of God (2 Thessalonians 2:4).

    2. He will promote or exalt himself above all other objects or forms of religious worship (2 Thessalonians 2:4).

    3. He will proclaim himself to be God as he sits in the temple of God (2 Thessalonians 2:4). Many Bible commentators believe this verse indicates that the original temple must be rebuilt on the temple mount now occupied by the Islamic Dome of the Rock.

    4. His presence will be attended with satanic power, false miraculous signs, lying wonders, and unrighteous deception that will be believed by those who are unsaved (2 Thessalonians 2:9–10).

  b. This is perhaps the most difficult interpretive question in 2 Thessalonians. There appear to be two possible answers: (1) The removal of civil government that will occur when the Antichrist sets himself up as the world dictator and (2) the departure of restraining presence of the Holy Spirit when the true church is raptured at the return of Jesus Christ (1 Thessalonians 4:13–18). This latter view seems to be the better one.

  c. The Antichrist will be consumed by words spoken by the Lord Jesus Christ and the brightness and radiance of His (Christ's) being (2 Thessalonians 2:8). This will happen when Christ returns to establish His reign/kingdom on earth.

5. They will be deceived by the Antichrist, believe the lies he will be promoting, and eventually perish (2 Thessalonians 2:10). Because these people did not receive the love of the truth, God will send them strong delusion that they might believe the lie (of Satan promoted through the Antichrist; 2 Thessalonians 2:11). They will be condemned by God to eternal damnation (2 Thessalonians 2:12).

6. a. Second Thessalonians 2:13 teaches that God chose us from the beginning through sanctification by the (Holy) Spirit and belief in the truth. This is perhaps the clearest verse in the Bible that explains the relationship of God's choosing individuals for salvation and the actual act of saving them. The Holy Spirit convicts the world/unsaved (John

16:7–11), some believe (not on their own, but as a response to the conviction of the Holy Spirit and sovereign grace offered to them by a loving God; Acts 16:30–31), and the Holy Spirit applies the washing and regeneration of the new birth, resulting in man's eternal salvation (Titus 3:5).

b. Man is called by/through the gospel of Jesus Christ, and the result is the obtaining of glory from Jesus Christ (2 Thessalonians 2:14).

7. God called or saved all Christians that they might receive God's glory. This probably means, among other things, that the original glory that was lost in the garden of Eden, is initially restored at salvation and ultimately restored when believers meet Christ (1 John 3:2).

8. a. Paul wanted the Thessalonians to stand fast and hold to the teachings he had given them. The phrase **stand fast** (NIV: "stand firm") means that the Thessalonian believers were not to give credence to unbelief or false doctrine, not even for one second.

b. Answers will vary.

9. a. God has given us His love, everlasting consolation, and good hope—all by grace. God has manifested His love toward Christians in a way that is tangible and experiential. God has given us everlasting consolation because He has solved the mystery of eternity for us. God has given us good hope because the best (eternity) is yet to come, and we have peace and a friend in Jesus who sticks closer than a brother.

b. God wants to comfort our hearts and establish and strengthen us in everything we do and say.

Lesson 9: Let the Word Run Swiftly

1. 1. Paul wanted the Thessalonians to pray that the word of God would spread rapidly (2 Thessalonians 3:1).

2. Paul wanted the Thessalonians to pray that the word of God would be glorified (2 Thessalonians 3:1).

3. He wanted the Thessalonians to pray that he and his missionary companions would be delivered from evil men (2 Thessalonians 3:2).

2. Answers will vary.

3. a. The phrase **as it is with you** provides the answer to this question. The word of God is glorified when an individual receives Jesus as Savior and Lord and allows the word of God to permeate and penetrate every aspect of his life. His life is lived as a reflection of God's grace, a living sacrifice for God's use, and a testimony to God's glory.
   b. Answers will vary.

4. Answers will vary.

5. God is faithful to His children and will guard you from the evil one/Satan and evil men (2 Thessalonians 3:3).

6. a. Paul said these believers were walking disorderly and being busybodies in the church (2 Thessalonians 3:7, 11).
   b. Their slothfulness was putting a financial burden on the rest of the church.
   c. Paul said he had not been disorderly when he was originally with them. He had not eaten anyone's bread without paying for it, and he had worked hard day and night (likely making tents; cf. Acts 18:3) so he could be an example of what it meant to work hard for the Lord.
   d. Answers will vary.

7. a. The Thessalonian believers were to withdraw or keep away from those who had previously been exhorted to work and refused to do so (2 Thessalonians 3:6, 14).
   b. They were to remember that those who were rejecting the truth, refusing to work and acting as busybodies were still brothers and sisters in Christ. Remembering this would help the Thessalonian believers not treat their sinning brothers and sisters as enemies.

8. a. Believers should examine their own hearts to see how they also have been tempted to fall into sin. If the believer does this honestly, he or she will see how easily someone else could enter into sin. This step of spiritual self-reflection will enable the believer to develop gentleness, which God will use to help restore the sinning believer.
   b. The Christian should go directly to the sinning believer to discuss the

matter (Matthew 18:15) with the goal of restoring him or her to spiritual fellowship with God. It's important to remember that the issue is sin, not a personal dislike for the person or a difference of personal convictions. The restoring believer shouldn't talk with others beforehand, which could lead to gossip and slander. If the sinning believer repents, he or she is won back to the Lord. If the sinning believer doesn't repent, the restoring believer takes one or two more believers (who act as witnesses) with him or her and attempts to help the sinning believer comprehend the seriousness of their sin and repent. If this second attempt is successful, the brother or sinner is won back to the Lord and the matter is settled. If the sinning believer is unrepentant, the restoring believer should bring the matter before the church and each member of the church should apply Galatians 6:1 and then go to the sinning believer (assumable one by one as the Lord leads them) with the goal of restoring the believer to the Lord. If the sinning believer doesn't listen to the church, the church is left with no alternative but to excommunicate the unrepentant believer. The church should always be willing to restore and receive the erring believer into fellowship based upon true repentance.

9. Answers will vary.

FINAL EXAM

Every person will eventually stand before God in judgment—the final exam. The Bible says, **And it is appointed for men to die once, but after this the judgment** (Hebrews 9:27).

May I ask you a question? *If you died today, do you know for certain you would go to heaven?* I did not ask if you're religious or a church member, nor did I ask if you've had some encounter with God—a meaningful spiritual experience. I didn't even ask if you believe in God or angels or if you're trying to live a good life. The question I *am* asking is this: *If you died today, do you know for certain you would go to heaven?*

When you die, you will stand alone before God in judgment. You'll either be saved for all eternity, or you will be separated from God for all eternity in what the Bible calls the lake of fire (Romans 14:12; Revelation 20:11–15). Tragically, many religious people who believe in God are not going to be accepted by Him when they die.

> **Many will say to Me in that day, "Lord, Lord, have we not prophesied in Your name, cast out demons in Your name, and done many wonders in Your name?" And then I will declare to them, "I never knew you; depart from Me, you who practice lawlessness!"** (Matthew 7:22–23)

God loves you and wants you to go to heaven (John 3:16; 2 Peter 3:9). If you are not sure where you'll spend eternity, you are not prepared to meet God. God wants you to know for certain that you will go to heaven.

> **Behold, now is the accepted time; behold, now is the day of salvation.** (2 Corinthians 6:2)

The words **behold** and **now** are repeated because God wants you to know that you can be saved today. You do not need to hear those terrible words, **Depart from Me ....** Isn't that great news?

Jesus himself said, **You must be born again** (John 3:7). These aren't the words of a pastor, a church, or a particular denomination. They're the words of Jesus Christ himself. You *must* be born again (saved from eternal damnation) before you die; otherwise, it will be too late when you die! You can know for certain today that God will accept you into heaven when you die.

These things I have written to you who believe in the name of the Son of God, that you may know *that you have eternal life.*

(1 John 5:13)

The phrase *you may know* means that you can know for certain before you die that you will go to heaven. To be born again, you must understand and accept four essential spiritual truths. These truths are right from the Bible, so you know you can trust them—they are not man-made religious traditions. Now, let's consider these four essential spiritual truths.

Essential Spiritual Truth

#1

The Bible teaches that you are a sinner and separated from God.

No one is righteous in God's eyes. To be righteous means to be totally without sin, not even a single act.

There is none righteous, no, not one;
There is none who understands;
There is none who seeks after God.
They have all turned aside;
They have together become unprofitable;
There is none who does good, no, not one.
(Romans 3:10–12)

...for all have sinned and fall short of the glory of God.
(Romans 3:23)

Look at the words God uses to show that all men are sinners—**none, not one, all turned aside, not one**. God is making a point: all of us are sinners. No one is good (perfectly without sin) in His sight. The reason is sin.

Have you ever lied, lusted, hated someone, stolen anything, or taken God's name in vain, even once? These are all sins.

Are you willing to admit to God that you are a sinner? If so, then tell Him right now you have sinned. You can say the words in your heart or aloud—it doesn't matter which—but be honest with God. Now check the box if you have just admitted you are a sinner.

☐ God, I admit I am a sinner in Your eyes.

Now, let's look at the second essential spiritual truth.

Essential Spiritual Truth

#2

The Bible teaches that you cannot save yourself or earn your way to heaven.

Man's sin is a very serious problem in the eyes of God. Your sin separates you from God, both now and for all eternity—unless you are born again.

For the wages of sin is death.
(Romans 6:23)

And you He made alive, who were dead in trespasses and sins.
(Ephesians 2:1)

Wages are a payment a person earns by what he or she has done. Your sin has earned you the wages of death, which means separation from God. If you die never having been born again, you will be separated from God after death.

You cannot save yourself or purchase your entrance into heaven. The Bible says that man is **not redeemed with corruptible things, like silver or gold** (1 Peter 1:18). If you owned all the money in the world, you still could not buy your entrance into heaven. Neither can you buy your way into heaven with good works.

For by grace you have been saved through faith, and that not of yourselves; it is the gift of God, not of works, lest anyone should boast. (Ephesians 2:8–9)

The Bible says salvation is **not of yourselves.** It is **not of works, lest anyone should boast.** Salvation from eternal judgment cannot be earned by doing good works; it is a gift of God. There is nothing you can do to purchase your way into heaven because you are already unrighteous in God's eyes.

If you understand you cannot save yourself, then tell God right now that you are a sinner, separated from Him, and you cannot save yourself. Check the box below if you have just done that.

☐ God, I admit that I am separated from You because of my sin. I realize that I cannot save myself.

Now, let's look at the third essential spiritual truth.

Essential Spiritual Truth

#3

The Bible teaches that Jesus Christ died on the cross to pay the complete penalty for your sin and to purchase a place in heaven for you.

Jesus Christ, the sinless Son of God, lived a perfect life, died on the cross, and rose from the dead to pay the penalty for your sin and purchase a place in heaven for you. He died on the cross on your behalf, in your place, as your substitute, so you do not have to go to hell. Jesus Christ is the only acceptable substitute for your sin.

For He [God, the Father] made Him [Jesus] who knew [committed] no sin to be sin for us, that we might become the righteousness of God in Him.
(2 Corinthians 5:21)

I [Jesus] am the way, the truth, and the life. No one comes to the Father except through Me.
(John 14:6)

Nor is there salvation in any other, for there is no other name under heaven given among men by which we must be saved.
(Acts 4:12)

Jesus Christ is your only hope and means of salvation. Because you are a sinner, you cannot pay for your sins, but Jesus paid the penalty for your sins by dying on the cross in your place. Friend, there is salvation in no one else—not angels, not some religious leader, not even your religious good works. No religious act such as baptism, confirmation, or joining a church can save you. There is no other way, no other name that can save you. Only Jesus Christ can save you. You must be saved by accepting Jesus Christ's substitutionary sacrifice for your sins, or you will be lost forever.

Do you see clearly that Jesus Christ is the only way to God in heaven? If you understand this truth, tell God that you understand, and check the box below.

☐ God, I understand that Jesus Christ died to pay the penalty for my sin. I understand that His death on the cross was the only acceptable sacrifice for my sin.

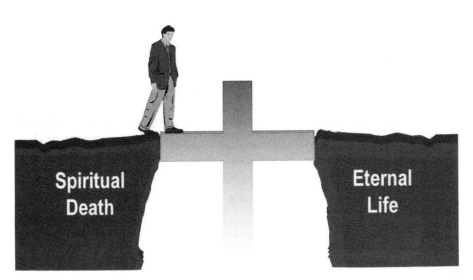

Essential Spiritual Truth

#4

By faith, you must trust in Jesus Christ alone for eternal life and call upon Him to be your Savior and Lord.

Many religious people admit they have sinned. They believe Jesus Christ died for the sins of the world, but they are not saved. Why? Thousands of moral, religious people have never completely placed their faith in Jesus Christ *alone* for eternal life. They think they must believe in Jesus Christ as a real person and do good works to earn their way to heaven. They are not trusting Jesus Christ *alone*. To be saved, you must trust in Jesus Christ *alone* for eternal life. Look what the Bible teaches about trusting Jesus Christ alone for salvation.

Believe on the Lord Jesus Christ, and you will be saved.
(Acts 16:31)

...that if you confess with your mouth the Lord Jesus and believe in your heart that God has raised Him from the dead, you will be saved. For with the heart one believes unto righteousness, and with the mouth confession is made unto salvation.... For there is no distinction between Jew and Greek, for the same Lord over all is rich to all who call upon Him. For "whoever calls on the name of the Lord shall be saved.
(Romans 10:9–10, 12–13)

Do you see what God is saying? To be saved or born again, you must trust Jesus Christ *alone* for eternal life. Jesus Christ paid for your complete salvation. Jesus said, **It is finished!** (John 19:30). Jesus paid for your salvation completely when He shed His blood on the cross for your sin.

If you believe that God resurrected Jesus Christ (proving God's acceptance of Jesus as a worthy sacrifice for man's sin) and you are willing to confess Jesus Christ as your Savior and Lord (master of your life), you will be saved.

Friend, right now God is offering you the greatest gift in the world. God wants to give you the *gift* of eternal life, the *gift* of His complete forgiveness for all your sins, and the *gift* of His unconditional acceptance into heaven when you die. Will you accept His free gift now, right where you are?

Are you unsure how to receive the gift of eternal life? Let me help you. Do you remember that I said you needed to understand and accept four essential spiritual truths? First, you admitted you are a sinner. Second, you admitted you were separated from God because of your sin and you could not save yourself. Third, you realized that Jesus Christ is the only way to heaven—no other name can save you.

Now, you must trust that Jesus Christ died once and for all to save your lost soul. Just take God at His word—He will not lie to you! This is the kind of simple faith you need to be saved. If you would like to be saved right now, right where you are, offer this prayer of simple faith to God. Remember, the words must come from your heart.

God, I am a sinner and deserve to go to hell. Thank You, Jesus, for dying on the cross for me and for purchasing a place in heaven for me. I believe You are the Son of God and You are able to save me right now. Please forgive me for my sin and take me to heaven when I die. I invite You into my life as Savior and Lord, and I trust You alone for eternal life. Thank You for giving me the gift of eternal life. Amen.

If, in the best way you know how, you trusted Jesus Christ alone to save you, then God just saved you. He said in His Holy Word, *But as many as received Him, to them He gave the right to become the children of God* (John 1:12). It's that simple. God just gave you the gift of eternal life by faith. You have just been born again, according to the Bible.

You will not come into eternal judgment, and you will not perish in the lake of fire—you are saved forever! Read this verse carefully and let it sink into your heart.

Most assuredly, I say to you, he who hears My word and believes in Him who sent Me has everlasting life, and shall not come into judgment, but has passed from death into life.
(John 5:24)

Now, let me ask you a few more questions.

According to God's holy Word (John 5:24), not your feelings, what kind of life did God just give you? _____

What two words did God say at the beginning of the verse to assure you that He is not lying to you? _____ _____

Are you going to come into eternal judgment? ☐ YES   ☐ NO

Have you passed from spiritual death into life? ☐ YES   ☐ NO

Friend, you've just been born again. You just became a child of God.

To help you grow in your new Christian life, we would like to send you some Bible study materials. To receive these helpful materials free of charge, e-mail your request to **info@LamplightersUSA.org.**

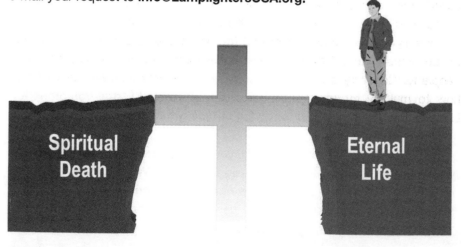

Spiritual Death

Eternal Life

Appendix

Level 1 (Basic Training)
Student Workbook

To begin, familiarize yourself with the Lamplighters' *Leadership Training and Development Process* (see graphic on page 104). Notice there are two circles: a smaller, inner circle and a larger, outer circle. The inner circle shows the sequence of weekly meetings beginning with an Open House, followed by an 8–14 week study, and concluding with a clear presentation of the gospel (Final Exam). The outer circle shows the sequence of the Intentional Discipleship training process (Leading Studies, Training Leaders, Multiplying Groups). As participants are transformed by God's Word, they're invited into a discipleship training process that equips them in every aspect of the intentional disciple-making ministry.

The Level 1 training (Basic Training) is *free*, and the training focuses on two key aspects of the training: 1) how to prepare a life-changing Bible study (ST-A-R-T) and 2) how to lead a life-changing Bible study (10 commandments). The training takes approximately 60 minutes to complete, and you complete it as an individual or collectively as a small group (preferred method) by inserting an extra week between the Final Exam and the Open House.

To begin your training, go to www.LamplightersUSA.org to register yourself or your group. A Lamplighters' Certified Trainer will guide you through the entire Level 1 training process. After you have completed the training, you can review as many times as you like.

When you have completed the Level 1 training, please consider completing the Level 2 (Advanced) training. Level 2 training will equip you to reach more people for Christ by learning how to train new leaders and by showing you how to multiply groups. You can register for additional training at www.LamplightersUSA.org.

Intentional Discipleship
Training & Development Process

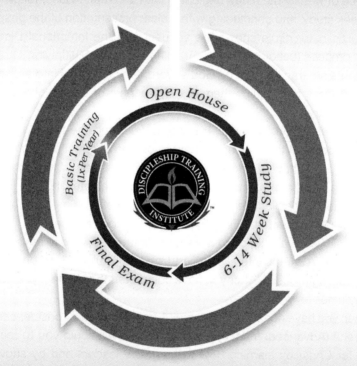

Multiplying Groups

The 5 Steps of Faith for Starting Studies

Training Library

Online Resources

Leading Studies

ST-A-R-T

10 Commandments

Solving All Group Problems

Open House

Basic Training (1x Per Year)

6-14 Week Study

Final Exam

Training Leaders

4 Responsibilities of a Trainer

Leadership Training

4 Levels of Student Development

3 Diagnostic Questions

John A. Stewart © 2017

How to Prepare a
Life-Changing Bible Study
ST-A-R-T

Step 1: _____ and _____.

Pray specifically for the group members and yourself as you study God's Word. Ask God (_____) to give each group member a rich time of personal Bible study, and thank (_____) God for giving you a desire to invest in the spiritual advancement of each other.

Step 2: _____ the _____.

Answer the questions in the weekly lessons without looking at the

_____ _____.

Step 3: _____and _____.

Review the Leader's Guide, and _____ every truth you missed when you originally did your lesson. Record the answers you missed with a _____ _____ so you'll know what you missed.

Step 4: _____ _____.

Calculate the specific amount of time _____ _____ to spend on each question and write the start time next to each one in the _____ using a _____.

How to Lead a Life-Changing Bible Study
10 COMMANDMENTS

1	2	3
4	5	6
7	8	9
	10	

Lamplighters' 10 Commandments are proven small group leadership principles that have been used successfully to train hundreds of believers to lead life-changing, intentional discipleship Bible studies.

Essential Principles for Leading Intentional Discipleship Bible Studies

1. The 1st Commandment: The _____ Rule.
   The Leader-Trainer should be in the room _____ minutes before the class begins.

2. The 2nd Commandment: The _____-_____ Rule.
   Train the group that it is okay to _____, but they should never be _____.

3. The 3rd Commandment: The _____ Rule.
   _____, _____, _____ ask for _____ to _____ the _____, _____, and _____ the questions. The Leader-Trainer, however, should always _____ the questions to control the _____ of the study.

4. The 4th Commandment: The ____:____ Rule.
   _____ the Bible study on time and _____ the study on time _____ _____. No exceptions!

5. The 5th Commandment: The _____ Rule.
   Train the group participants to _____ on God's Word for answers to life's questions.

1	2	3
4 **59:59**	5	6
7	8	9
	10	

6. The 6th Commandment: The _____ Rule.
   Deliberately and progressively _____ _____ participants into the group discussion over a period of time.

7. The 7th Commandment: The _____ _____ Rule.
   _____ the participants to get _____ the answers to the questions, not just _____ or _____ ones.

8. The 8th Commandment: The _____ Rule.
   _____ the group discussion so you _____ the lesson _____ _____ and give each question _____ _____.

9. The 9th Commandment: The _____-_____ Rule.
   Don't let the group members talk about _____
   _____, _____ _____, or
   _____ _____.

10. The 10th Commandment: The _____ Rule.
    _____ God to change lives, including _____.

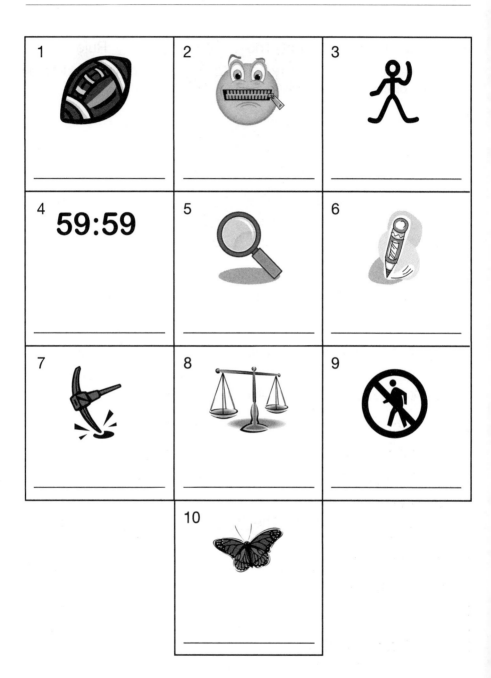

Choose your next study from any of the following titles

- John 1-11
- John 12-21
- Acts 1-12
- Acts 13-28
- Romans 1-8
- Romans 9-16
- Galatians
- Ephesians
- Philippians

- Colossians
- 1 & 2 Thessalonians
- 1 Timothy
- 2 Timothy
- Titus/Philemon
- Hebrews
- James
- 1 Peter
- 2 Peter/Jude

Additional Bible studies and sample lessons are available online.

For audio introductions on all Bible studies, visit us online at www.Lamplightersusa.org.

Looking to begin a new group?
The Lamplighters Starter Kit includes:

- 8 James Bible Study Guides (students purchase their own books)
- 25 Welcome Booklets
- 25 Table Tents
- 25 Bible Book Locator Bookmarks
- 50 Final Exam Tracts
- 50 Invitation Cards

For a current listing of live and online discipleship training events, or to register for discipleship training, go to www.LamplightersUSA.org/training.